THE MISTRESS CONTRACT

THE MISTRESS CONTRACT

BY SHE AND HE

UNBRIDLED BOOKS

Unbridled Books

Copyright © 2011

Library of Congress Cataloging-in-Publication Data
    The mistress contract / by She and He.
        p.   cm.
    ISBN 978-1-60953-064-8
    1. Mistresses.   2. Man-woman relationships.
HQ806.M585 2011
813'.6—dc22   2011019932

1   3   5   7   9   10   8   6   4   2

Book Design by SH • CV

First Printing

CONTRACT

1. This Contract is for mistress services to be performed by Ms. ███████████ for Mr. ███████████.

2. The compensation for these services shall be at whatever amount is required to provide Ms. ███████████ tasteful accommodations to her liking together with expenses accrued in the normal course of her activities.

3. In return for this compensation, Ms. ███████████ will provide the following mistress services:

   a. Companionship for Mr. ███████████ when he is in the area, unless Ms. ███████████ is indisposed or traveling.

   b. All sexual acts engaged in when requested by Mr. ███████████, with suspension of historical, emotional, psychological disclaimers for duration of time requested, to be determined by Mr. ███████████.

      For duration of Agreement, Ms. ███████████ becomes sexual property of Mr. ███████████.

Ms. ___███████████___

Mr. ___███████████___

Date: ___███████████___

BED

Scene: HE and SHE in bed with tape recorder.

Time: A night in April, in California in the 1980s.

She: Sometime we're going to have to talk on tape about this agreement we've signed.

He: The content of these tapes should appear in a book, and if the content is as outrageous as the contract, it's going to outrage some people. We will need to hire someone to transcribe and edit the tapes.

She: It has to be someone we trust absolutely because the first thing they will need to do is to remove anything that could identify us and make sure that it never sees the light of day.

He: Ok, ok, one thing I find fascinating, and which makes me fall in love with you every time I think of it, is . . . where did you get the audacity (I wouldn't call it courage) to try something like that? The sheer genius? When I go back over all of our arguments, all the times when we were thrashing about on the issue of your bending your will to another,

other figures loomed up, shadows from the past. If we did something together, all the other men you'd done it with interposed themselves. . . .

Thoughts on Dialogue

She: We began our recording of conversations on Saturday after buying a Sony tape recorder that could fit in my purse. I felt strengthened by the device. We tried it first in Hilary's for coffee, and it sucked up our words in spite of a speaker on the wall nearby, and we continued later at the same place for dinner— many guests, yet the words fairly clear. Over dinner, our words gradually became slurred with wine, and often our mouths were full.

I have transcribed one tape. What emerges:

1. He is fluent, pedantic, complex-compound, archaically eloquent, long-winded, and occasionally—when he switches to simple diction—comical. He dominates the conversation by his flow, but it is apparent that the subject interests him, that he has many thoughts on male-female boundaries and wishes to understand. He listens.

2. I am much less skilled at speaking and confine myself to that which I feel or know, or think I know. Several times I confess to feeling confused about where we are going and say so. We get back on target.

Telephone

She: I find it fascinating. Hair-raising. The airy reaches of abstraction and the hawk plummet down to what we're doing in bed. It's exciting.

He: Yes, it is. When we're in bed.

She: Not talking about it?

He: Yes, it's very titillating. I've got an erection right now.

She: I spent a long time at the bookstore today. I can't cover the literature. There's no way I'm going to read all that stuff. Just in that one little tiny mall bookstore, there were three my-height shelves filled with books on relationships between the sexes.

This one probably won't make a dime. We'll do it anyway.

He: There's nothing like this. Psychologists, relationships, and therapists. Psychologists are so tedious.

She: Also I read last night a good bit of the Comfort book. I can't read that stuff too closely. But I had the terrible feeling reading it that you have been underprivileged and that I must do something about it.

He: I don't read that stuff, so I wouldn't know whether I'm underprivileged or not.

She: The woman is supposed to be a lecher and a temptress. I've tried to puzzle out why I never have been.

He: You've never had to be.

She: We should pretend.

He: Fine.

She: So that you'll get your due.

He: How come you haven't ever read that stuff before?

She: I don't enjoy it. It's not literature. I'm feeling like an investigative reporter. I'm going to hound you. I'm going to dig right into it and get you to discuss at every point. I feel that I have a new sense attached, my little machine. The restaurant tape is funny. Our speech begins to get fuzzy, and sometimes our mouths are full. It's gross.

He: Yes, indeed, you've got a wonderful little machine. Love you, sweetheart.

She: Bye-bye, dear.

HILARY'S RESTAURANT

She: You will be asking the lead questions because you are trying to understand how your view of women has changed in recent . . .

He: . . . just two weeks ago . . . damn right . . .

She: You have the feeling that change has taken place with great rapidity?

He: That's true. This all began when I began to puzzle about your reticence in telling me about yourself. You never minded telling me about your moods. I got quite enough of your moods. You would tell me about your ideas, but you never told me about your body—how it reacted or got upset, its likes and dislikes. You would only convey that by indirection. You would indicate displeasure when something occurred that you didn't like, and sometimes you would indicate pleasure when something occurred that you did like, but because of the basic perversity of your nature, one could never learn from that. One had only to repeat something in bed to find that it caused you displeasure. And you simply took no responsibility. You thought, I presume, all men were clods, and, that being the case, how could you possibly convey anything to them? Certainly you never took any responsibility in helping me, or any male, change his behavior.

She: There is a male mystique. I assume men are fragile. They need to believe that their techniques are sufficient, and if the woman doesn't swoon, she's not swoon material, is frigid. I've heard many men state flatly that this or that woman "is not good in bed." Remember that phrase? You'd best not tamper with what he presents to you, or he may fall apart or become angry or walk away. Anything could happen.

He: I don't really understand that at all.

She: There's a reluctance to talk about those things which should be mysterious, unspoken.

He: Why? We sometimes talk about ideas, a mystery wrapped in enigma, the concept of the Trinity as a mystery wrapped in enigma. . . .

She: It certainly is.

He: It is indeed mysterious that it took me fifty-five years of being conscious of females and wanting to know all about them to find out some of the most basic things about their anatomy.

She: You possibly weren't curious. You knew what you wanted. What basic things.

He: Such as the physiology of the orgasm, that even though an organ might be sensitive at Time A, isn't sensitive at Time B and vv. The fact that the clitoris might be sensitive at one time, oversensitive at another, and not sensitive at all other times.

She: You must have been monstrously inattentive. Certainly from trial and error, experimentation, you knew some of that before Kinsey told you.

He: I'm sorry, but I disagree with you. I'm sure some very sensitive females . . . women who were willing to observe their own responses . . . could have solved those problems for me very readily. If there's any mystique, it's the female's mystique of maleness and the female's unwillingness to be candid, or to say, "No, that doesn't feel good."

She: I'm sure that if you had touched a clitoris attached to a female and it had been unpleasant, she'd have let you know, somehow. It can be extremely unpleasant.

He: I realize that, but it would take a male an incredible amount of time to discover when it is and when it isn't. The defense of saying "Well, I don't like to be directive or attack the male ego" is an excuse for undergoing pain. Talk about double messages . . . quintuple, octuple, sextuple! The messages are so confusing that it would take a very astute male, one willing to expend an enormous amount of energy, to learn the female anatomy. And that brings up a philosophical problem. No one can get into another person's mind even if you're the best hermeneutics expert in the world. That is impossible. I cannot feel your pain. I cannot feel your pleasure. The only thing another person can do is observe physical states of being, and if you fail to connect those states of being to precise behavior on the part of another human being, obviously that shows. You'll get thirty years of failure to communicate.

She: The woman may also, by not pointing out to him what hurts and what's boring, what's irritating, get herself a husband . . . someone who will help her get along in life. In 1950 (I can't speak for the other women), I would not have said, "What you're doing hurts."

He: But even now, you can tell me what hurts, but it's very difficult, in fact impossible, for you to tell me what pleases you. . . .

She: But if I tell you what pleases me, you might do it a second or third time, the next night, maybe. I've known men like that. . . .

He: Well, you could say, "I don't feel like that. . . . I want to do something else."

She: But then I have taken over the direction, and I don't want that.

He: Well, neither do I.

She: Neither of us does. So what do we do about that?

He: You say to me, in effect, "Well, you have such a simple-minded anatomy, it doesn't make any difference. I know there are always fifteen things I can do that will please you, and if it's the same thing every night for fifteen years, you'd be satisfied.

She: I never said or thought that.

He: It's the way you behave.

She: In other words, you don't like what I've been doing. You wish I'd do something else. . . .

He: No—what I'm saying is that you've considered me and all other males easily satisfied. They aren't complex, so you take really very little interest in their anatomy or what pleases them or doesn't please them because they seem so aggressive, so 'linear,' as you would say.

She: Anything that takes about five hours a day is not easy. If their satisfaction takes five hours out of every twenty-four, it must not be very simple.

He: I don't understand . . . male satisfaction? Five hours? Most males, you said, come to orgasm in thirty seconds.

She: Not the ones I've known. The men in the books—the statistical, so-called average males—are speedy.

He: Now, that's not the case with me any longer. There's only one male that you've spent that much time in bed with, day after day after day. . . .

She: Well, you would have, at the same age as he. . . .

He: The point is, I didn't know you then.

She: The point is, they're not easily satisfied.

He: Satiated.

She: Or satiated.

He: But they can repeat the same act endlessly, and it's pretty acceptable. . . .

She: Apparently. But not for me.

He: That's right. But I'm telling you that's your view of males. They aren't complicated. They aren't complex. They're gross, unseemly. . . .

She: No, merely focused, as I am not.

He: Well, let me put it this way. They're simple mechanisms compared with the complexity of females. Now, that's something you really believe.

She: Having most of the equipment on the outside, rather than the inside, having most of the locus of pleasure in one place rather than spread throughout the body, makes it simpler.

He: It does.

She: You agree?

He: Well, simpler, as one would say, in this day and age, on one level. It may *seem* simpler, but beneath that rough exterior lies a sensitive heart.

She: I had a hell of a time getting rid of C. And other men have stuck around.

He: Yes, they tend to stick around.

She: So . . . I must be doing something that they like.

He: Yes, but you have very attractive equipment.

She: O, come, now!

He: One vagina is not like another. One body doesn't smell like another. One pair of hands doesn't move like another. There are all sorts of things you do that arouse men. You don't even know you do them.

She: (*Laughter*) So you think I should bring all this to a conscious level? What were we talking about? We were going to bring you into . . .

He: . . . into the modern world, learning to deal with feminism, the new consciousness. It all began when I was puzzled that we've been together, so to speak, forever, and you've *never* told me anything about your feelings, the indifference of your vagina, unless . . . (you've a new term) and unless you've been aroused to the plateau.

She: That's not a new term. I knew that in 1947? I read books in 1947. It was in van de Velde . . . called *Ideal Marriage* . . . in plain print.

He: I didn't read van de Velde. I don't read sex books or marriage manuals.

She: But I would have known it even if I hadn't read van de Velde. And reading at least one manual might have given you some knowledge which you claim you've lacked.

He: You have not instructed me at all. For all these years, you have been absolutely irresponsible. You've looked at me as a source of pleasure, and when I didn't give it to you, you put me down as a clod, insensitive. . . .

She: I haven't!

He: Yes, you have. Obviously I didn't understand you, and you have dissembled, you have feigned orgasms, feigned pleasure. . . .

She: No!

He: Yes, and you've done things to me that you didn't like to do, and you didn't indicate that this was not pleasing to you.

She: But you present yourself to a female as if sure you

know all, and if you don't, just going in and out will at least provide you with pleasant sensations.

He: I haven't behaved that way since I was in my forties, when we first constituted this . . . relationship.

She: All right, but at that age you brought to my bed not just yourself and your body but a whole reputation and myth, a hands-off myth.

He: I don't mind your believing in a Jamesian apperceptive mass, but what really annoys me is that you won't allow anyone to escape from one's past.

She: It would have taken a great deal of courage at our age then for me to receive a man who has been playing women, controlling women, moving them and moving on, and not letting them know what he was about, and not letting them see what hurt him or upset him . . . to take a man like that and say, "What you just did is unpleasant for me," or "Why don't you make love another way? It would please me more." It would have been impossible for me to have said that to you. You would have gone out the garage door (that room where we began).

He: I would not.

She: I thought you would have.

He: I am a learner. I *love* to learn.

She: Anyway, it was all completely pleasing to me at that time.

He: I see. As you changed, though, you didn't clue me in.

She: Until quite recently, I was never with you long

enough. If you'll remember, during the years when we were concerned with getting custody of my children, etc., our times together were not long enough . . .

He: . . . or placid enough . . .

She: . . . to concern ourselves with lovemaking.

He: So these conversations are a real luxury, a psychic luxury.

She: Yes, they come after we've ceased to be an active mother and father.

He: So young people couldn't do this. This is a contribution to understanding what our mature years can make.

She: I don't agree. I think young people are now doing this. It's a different generation.

He: Has it been recorded anywhere?

She: The men are now different.

He: They are? They are not like me. Is that right?

She: They speak very directly to each other, particularly the women to the men. And then if speaking and practicing doesn't help, they talk of the spark which is not there, and they give it up. And go off in different directions.

He: I see. Well, that's very wise of them.

She: We need to ask the questions which come from the question behind all others: What do we know, now, about women and men? Anything?

He: I told you that when I was at the beach in the rain today, when I thought about it, it was mainly a rush of emotion, and I could not articulate that emotion. Rather, I just stumbled along the beach wondering what I was feeling. Our conversation this noon drove questions out of my mind. The only thing I thought of was the fact that, thinking of our children, it might be the case that a dialogue between young couples run in this manner could be just as valuable as between ourselves.

She: By doing this, recording it and publishing it, we might be giving a novel method to other people. Perhaps one of the routes through the current Sturm und Drang of the feminist movement is for couples to discuss in a very methodical manner all of the issues which presumably we'll raise in the course of these conversations.

He: Yes, I think you're right, but I also think they have other ways than those which were available to us.

She: They're more used to talking to each other. They are less committed to a lifelong partner.

He: Or to an affirmation of their sex.

She: They don't seem to be as frightened of losing the one love.

He: I see. You're saying that younger people are better able to communicate.

She: I don't *know* that this is so. . . .

He: I don't agree. I find them much less articulate than our generation, much less capable of forming distinctions, particularly philosophical distinctions, of being able to distinguish a philosophical from a psychological issue, or for that matter being able to distinguish social, economic, political, philosophical, and psychological issues. They tend to be muddleheaded. I question whether the younger generation has sufficient command of the language to carry out an adequate dialogue which will provide them with any insight. You cannot think if you cannot express your thought. You can feel, but you cannot think.

She: I think that's poppycock. They are great believers in jumping into doing and leaving the words behind. Do it and see what happens. They have the language but feel that language is illusory.

He: One thinks what one says. One doesn't always have to use a social language such as English or French. You can think in all sorts of languages, but you must be able to *express* it in language, mathematics, music, logic, symbolism of some kind, or a social language. And obviously the subject we're discussing is amenable to examination only through a social language, not through music, not through symbolic logic, mathematics, physics, or chemistry—or any of those languages.

She: It is also possible merely to try to change behavior. Perhaps, through use of a drug . . .

He: Well, I could use a cattle prod to change your behavior very easily. I could use operant conditioning. For instance . . . take your most recent hang-up, and that is sucking me. Because you couldn't stand to suck C., every time you approach a penis, all of those things well up in our mind.

Not only in your mind, your throat and everyplace else. Now, I could use any number of techniques of behavior modification and deal with the problem, but I would much prefer to deal with it on a philosophical level because I think it's more profound, less manipulative, and ultimately more satisfactory. Lots of psychologists will disagree with me.

She: Dealing with it on a philosophical level would mean what?

He: The lecture I gave you last night on existentialism when you brought up the importance of the meaning of existence. . . .

She: I want to go back to that and interrupt you. Your definition or presentation of existentialism doesn't mean anything to me. I don't know what you're talking about. When men deliver lectures . . .

He: Let me put it this way . . .

She: Let me finish my sentence. You gave a lecture last night on existentialism, and I responded by saying to you, "This is my present. My present condition is: When I am asked to suck, when it is conveyed to me . . .

He: You're not asked very often . . .

She: . . . that that would be desired, my existence at that moment is that I wonder why you like it so much. I wonder why I have been doing it all these years. I wonder if there is anything more useless to me and at the same time more pleasurable to you. I wonder what my vagina is for. And so forth. That's what my existence is at that moment. It has very little to do with previous malfeasance, with ex-husband.

He: But that's what you said last night.

She: I told you last night of one particular occurrence of force used, which floods back on me, but so do other thoughts, and it's hard for me to turn off any of those thoughts.

He: You seem to equate the zombie-like response of the stranger in Camus with existentialism, as though that is what existentialism is all about—to be a zombie. All of the philosophers of existentialism were vibrant men, sexually, socially . . . you could take all the logical positivists, all the philosophers of the world, roll them up, and they wouldn't make one Camus.

She: I agree. I don't know anything about it, but I agree anyway.

He: You have taken the negation of existentialism as the message, whereas the message is that you have that choice. You can be a zombie, or you can be totally involved in our present existence. Like Camus or Sartre. You have simply fallen into a philosophical misapprehension which comes from lack of intellectual discipline.

She: At the moment it is happening, what am I supposed to do with all the thoughts? They are there. Like Camus's stranger, I am the passive recipient of male plans and am surrounded at such times by a feeling that I've not been consulted, am, in fact, nobody.

He: The point is, you haven't decided what it is you really

want. If you really want to avoid that act and to establish all relationships with males *ex* that act, that's how you should act. You should not pretend. You should assert, "This is the price of admission into my intimacy. If you want anything else, then go someplace else."

She: I should know whether I feel strongly enough.

He: Yes, you should know that.

She: Often the fact that he wants something so alien to me is enough. . . .

He: You feel strongly enough about it to make that issue, every time it arises, as unpleasant as possible.

She: Not *every* time.

He: Ninety-nine percent. You make it so unpleasant that there should be a cessation of all such activities. You make it into a federal case every time it occurs. You raise the issue of the vagina, and I could screw you a hundred times, as I have, then ask you to suck me once, and you would immediately say, "What have I got a vagina for?" A thousand times. And because I ask you to do this once, you imply that I've asked you to do it every time. You have challenged the very nature of my sexuality.

She: The issue of the vagina is a logical dodge. I raised it precisely because I don't want to challenge the nature of your sexuality. What an uproar that would be. It should be simple to say to a man, "Look—my throat is too small, my taste is for celery and peanut butter, not semen, and I'm a nervous vomiter." And I should be able to say, "It *can't* be the nature of your sexuality to wish to place your generative organ down my throat!" But as I say, men are fragile. It's hard for me to think of myself, after all these years, as suddenly a totally ungenerous lover. But perhaps I never was generous.

He: I think you think of yourself as a cafeteria. The choices are there, and the customer can choose so long as he takes only the things that are there.

She: Every male, with one exception, has asked for sucking. Not only asked for it but considered it to be the highest, most perfect pleasure.

He: Now you're falling into . . .

She: Let me finish—which puts into a strange perspective all the ways of lovemaking.

He: When you say "every male"—do you include me in that?

She: Yes. When, out of necessity, I left your locale, you made not frequent but greatly looked-forward-to visits. We communicated by telephone once a week. When you got off the plane, you always said you were tired, tired. You usually drove my car sixty miles to where I lived. Often you pulled out your penis (in the car) and said, "Suck me." What I'd been doing or thinking, what I was feeling, you didn't ask. You said, "Do it." You didn't ask me whether I wanted to.

He: And then when we got home, I made love to you all night.

She: No, when we got home, you spoke with the children, and then you went to bed and slept because you were so tired. In the middle of the night, we made love. Intimacy to you was one thing, to me another.

He: We wanted antithetical things. You would say you wanted companionship with breakfast, long walks, a sense of intimacy. I wanted sex. In all shapes, sizes, and varieties. An exchange between individuals can be considered as a marketplace in which individuals exchange those things that they have for what they want. If each person had the same things and wanted the same things, there would be no exchange. For instance, *now*, for sex, I bring financial rewards, a sense of the involvement with the external world, maybe some sort of excitement, and you bring sensitivity, involvement with the arts, three lovely children, apperceptive mass. Those are exchanges and bargains made. Negotiations entered into, and every once in a while you say, "No, no, no—this isn't right at all. This isn't what I really think the relationship between a man and a woman should be. It should be all breakfasts and walks."

She: (*Laughter*) In my life, I have had the feeling that there would be no breakfasts and no walks if one had sex *first*.

He: Well, I have never felt that way at all about breakfast or walks or sex. Breakfasts and walks always seemed like a good postlude. There's nothing wrong with that.

She: But the only way of holding you to the walks is to delay the sex.

He: I guess what is emerging is the fact that you perceive sex as your sole bargaining piece—not your wit, your charm, that you are capable of delightful conversation and anyone would look forward to your company.

She: That's something I've learned from males. I've learned what they want the most. They value sex. They don't value wit, etc.

He: If you read about men who were obviously fascinating as personalities, you will usually find a female that fascinated them.

She: Certainly Jane did not fascinate Carlyle.

He: Carlyle, if he spoke as he wrote, was a colossal bore. But I'm thinking of men of action—Napoleon, Caesar, Pompey, Alexander, Anthony, Roosevelt, Kennedy, Johnson. Certainly Lady Bird was someone who fascinated him and kept him interested. And most fascinating men have fascinating women. Being dull isn't a necessary attribute of being female.

She: They "have" fascinating women and then go elsewhere.

He: You exhibit the overt characteristics of helplessness.

She: That's true.

He: That is boring, very boring.

She: I've lost track of where we're going. We're wandering too far afield. I feel I *never* have been timed with a man in everyday living.... Once bed is over, they have other things to do. They value me only for that, and they want to do other things with all the time that's left. They go on to things which are by definition more valuable. Business, money.

He: You have never lived in daily pleasant concourse with a man?

She: With Billy E., perhaps. He continually asked, as I've told you, what do men and women *do* with each other all that time? You can only spend so much time in bed, and all the rest of the time—how do they spend it?

He: Of course, I think they ought to spend it working. Man is a working animal.

She: And woman? It's immensely sad to rub, touch, writhe, moan, and then get up, notice it's a beautiful day, and he departs. It's depressing.

He: How does one earn a living?

She: There's something about the economy of time. One should spend more time on other forms of intimacy.

He: When you had three children . . .

She: I didn't want any of my time with my children to be spent *frivolously* with an insatiable husband.

He: And that would have been true of me if I had been your husband?

She: Probably. With the children, time was so intimate, so rewarding and close and meaningful. The energy exchange with them never happened with men.

He: Never?

She: Never.

He: You should have stayed pregnant all your life.

She: Unfortunately, it was hard on me.

He: Why don't you live with women with small children and devote your life to that?

She: Because there's a distancing as your body becomes older and you're no longer capable of conceiving. You're looking at children through the wrong end of a telescope. They're far away, and that's as it should be. It's nature's way of preparing you for something different.

He: I'm wondering about what you've said and what impact that would have on a relationship with a male. As you've described it, it would be impossible for you to go through childbearing and child-rearing and emerge with an intact relationship with a male.

She: Yes. In the current literature about motherhood and mothering (which is no longer ecstatic nor as plump with the myth of the ecstasy of nurturing), you will find an awareness that not only are mothers not saints and mothering not the saintliest of occupations, but also the women are recording that they are not much interested in what is happening with their husbands. They feel at a dreadful distance from their husbands, and not everyone can be included.

He: You can't blame the male for not finding that very satisfactory.

She: No, you can't blame them.

He: You would have left [C.] even if he'd been a saint.

24

She: On the contrary, I think that if he'd shifted his emphasis from the bed to a shared daily life ... cared for the children, widened his focus, etc. ... then the intimacy would have grown.

He: No. Had you had your druthers, you would have simply stopped sexual intercourse. If I had been married to you at forty and you had done that, the result would have been inevitable. I'd have left you. I'd have left you at fifty. At sixty.

She: That's a crux, huh? What the women may be asking the men to do is unacceptable to them, and I can understand that. But you're putting it rather extremely. Celibacy is extreme.

He: It's clearly what you would have preferred.

She: Preferred when going to bed with him didn't interest me too much.

He: It wouldn't have interested you if you'd been living with Don Giovanni.

She: Don Giovanni would have been no contest with children. It's a very trite complaint, but I was ... overextended, physically.

He: Aren't most women?

She: With three children? Yes, they are.

He: It seems to me that a woman's sexuality ebbs and flows like tides, not only on a daily, monthly basis, but also in stages. Male sexuality rises sharply, peaks at about eighteen, and then is slow and steady until death, is constant, unvaried, or seldom varies, and if it varies it's because of external environment, not internal environment. Male sexuality is not generally affected by endocrine changes after puberty.

She: It is affected by the mate's response.

He: The sociobiologists are right in their conclusions, perhaps wrong in their argument. Very simply, out of that irregularity versus regularity, the satisfaction of male sexual needs requires multiple partners, whereas the satisfaction of female sexual needs requires occasional partners, or at intervals, but not regularly or constantly.

She: Again, I don't know about my sisters. . . .

He: We're just talking about you as the paradigm of all women.

She: I don't know who elected me paradigm of all women. I know that I would have been much relieved if I'd been allowed by my society to dispense with men for long periods of time while I was doing other things which required my mind and body.

He: Pregnancy and child-rearing requires a physical commitment that no male could possibly understand. If I were put out of commission for nine bloody months . . .

She: That's not necessarily the case.

He: No, but hauling around a big belly, given my attitude, I probably would have stabbed it.

She: No—you wouldn't have.

He: And then hauling a child around at my breast. I would view the world in an entirely different manner!

She: Yes. Your heart stops when they're in danger, you're deeply relieved when they're happy. It's an emotional roller coaster all day long every day. At least it was for me. Then the husband comes home, and he wants sport. You are exhausted, and even with the best of intentions, the transition to him is not easy. He wants dinner and wash-up and listen-to-him. Make love and then answer the cry of the baby. We know all the difficulties, and I don't have any solution.

He: Those difficulties have been glossed over in a thousand marriage manuals, and maybe it's absolutely irrelevant in that society does not require that male and female inhabit one household throughout a period of time. It's also very possible that societies which have provided houses of prostitution and all sorts of things which the feminists think degrading and inhuman indeed protect a large portion of females. In that regard, it's quite possible that prostitutes sustain the sacrifice that one group of females demands of another, which will allow them to go forward with child-rearing, household-keeping, society maintenance. This has been true for centuries. You wouldn't sacrifice your sisters, but it's possible it's not a sacrifice. In some respects, in some periods, being a prostitute might have a lot of advantages that childbearing and all the other things don't have. Perhaps the trade-off is not as unequal as it seems nor the degradation as gross as it seems.

She: I believe prostitution is degrading for everyone.

He: What is the male to do if he is sensitive to the female

and she says, "For the next five years, I don't want to screw you"?

She: She doesn't say that.

He: Now, listen—he's sensitive. He isn't Torwald in *Nora* or Charles in *Emma*. He is aware that Nora has three kids and doesn't want to screw Torwald. Nora had help with the children. She just thought Torwald was a jerk. Many women get very lonely, distracted, upset, and almost crazy spending all their time with three children. But Nora didn't want Torwald's body. She wanted his companionship. Now, let's say Torwald is not a Norwegian slob but a perceptive human being, and he gives Nora companionship for five years, or longer . . .

She: With occasional . . .

He: No, not at all.

She: Nothing? Pretty extreme.

He: Not at all. Nora, in her heart of hearts, would like to put that out of her consciousness for five years, not deal with it. What's he going to do during these five years?

She: But she will not put him out for five years. She allows him in.

He: I'm dealing with a situation in which Nora does not want to have communication with her husband for five years. I'm sure this occurs in millions of instances.

She: Most women would say that they feel deeply comforted by the husband's presence.

He: I'm not saying that she doesn't want companionship, doesn't want to be comforted.

She: Forget Nora and Torwald. He's impossible, and so is she.

He: How is a man to achieve those physical satisfactions he needs during the five years with his wife's child bearing?

She: You're assuming that males are totally different from females and they *must* have it.

He: Yes, I'll tell you they do. If I couldn't, I'd join a monastery or become queer or I'd get other women, but I wouldn't merely sit there for five years. There's no way on God's green earth that I would refrain. I wouldn't at sixty. At thirty, I would have clawed the walls.

She: It would make you unhealthy, is that right?

He: Listen, at thirty—and that's when most men are siring children—if I couldn't screw five times a day . . .

She: *Five times a day!*

He: That's right. I'd have been out of my goddamn mind!

She: Maybe you belong in an insane asylum. Why would anyone want to screw five times a day? That's ridiculous. No wonder you didn't do anything significant until you were forty. You're monstrous.

He: But I could have done it all at night.

She: With someone who has cared for children all day long . . . ?

He: Well, I too worked all day long. . . .

She: How long were each of the five?

He: O, maybe fifteen minutes. I could control myself so that one time could be thirty minutes or an hour.

She: Congratulations. Did the women like it?

He: I didn't ask. I'm merely reporting. You want this to be a candid exchange, do you not?

She: I'm certainly glad I met you at forty-two because I can't think of anything more tedious than spending that much time *not* out walking, not sleeping. . . .

He: In the depth of night, you aren't going to be out walking.

She: Many's the walk we have taken.

He: Five times isn't very much.

She: Five times is monstrously much.

He: You do it when you get home. You do it three times at night and once in the morning.

She: O, God . . .

He: Well, am I to tell you that I don't want to screw five times a day?

She: Of course not.

He: And I didn't look at myself as having any particular sexual prowess. It just seemed normal to me.

She: Why would it seem normal to you when the females probably didn't think it was all that desirable?

He: I never asked!

She: Because you're a clod. If she wanted to have you around, she had to submit to this.

He: That's true.

She: And you ignored all the rest of her.

He: No, that's not true.

She: You didn't have *time* to pay any attention to anything else. And I'll bet, as soon as you finished, you went to a tome on logical positivism, or to sleep, or food, or talked on the telephone. Until she passed by and you said, "O, by the way, what are we having for dinner tonight?" or "Let me see, how would you like a little nooky?"

He: That's probably true. I don't think I was extreme.

She: I think you were extreme. I think you're braggin'.

He: No, I'm not.

She: Yes, you are.

He: Well, at twenty-five, how about your ex?

She: Both of you were monsters.

He: C. didn't brag about it.

She: Certainly he did.

He: Now, really, please, the Kinsey Report is full of instances like myself and your ex.

She: It's a bell-shaped curve. You admit that? And you are way out at one end.

He: The thing I find interesting with you is that you know so many men at both ends of the bell-shaped curve and not in the middle.

She: No, only at the monster end.

He: G. wasn't a monster.

She: He was in the middle. He was the only one, and I never went back.

He: So you had one instance, and you said, "I don't like that" and went to the other extreme. What does that tell you about you? What is it about men like C. and myself that you like? There must be something about us that you find appealing. The two most important men in your life. Isn't that true? You know the answer. It's just complicated.

She: I like intellectually complicated, thinking men.

He: Most thoughtful, thinking men don't have that characteristic which you dislike. Wanting to screw all day.

She: It's as my son said: "It isn't that I like big-breasted women. It's that they like me!"

He: So you were the innocent victim.

She: I don't know. I don't know how passive I am.

He: Don't you think it's strange that you've ended up with men like that?

She: If you're going to turn around now and call it an attraction, no one is going to believe us.

He: An attraction . . . ?

She: . . . between this woman who would like to declare periods of celibacy and men who like to screw five times a day.

He: Therein might lie, in an extreme example, a paradigm of male-female conflict. The male-female conflict might be best arrived at in an instance of a relationship with one female who would want five years of celibacy, who attracts or is attracted by males who want to screw five times a day. Now, *there* is a major disjuncture. I think that what we need to do is to get to the bottom of this.

She: (*Laughter*)

He: Don't you? Certainly our children would appreciate it if we did.

DINNER

She: I want to tell you about something which is probably solely a female experience.

He: There are a lot of them, like childbirth, suckling.

She: This is something that happens after the childbirth years, and probably only to women.

He: There is no such thing as a male menopause.

She: There isn't?

He: I don't know—I'm commenting on things that can only happen to women.

She: You'll have to tell me if I'm wrong. Maybe it could happen to a man.

He: Is it anatomically possible?

She: It's not sociologically possible.

He: If it's anatomically possible, then . . .

She: You don't know what I'm talking about.

He: It's like Twenty Questions.

She: I have this friend, J. He teaches out at the school. He's a musician. He's twenty-five years old, and it happens that he and I are capable of talking sensibly about a lot of issues, and we merely tolerate the rest of the folk out of school. He's a graduate in art history. He's lively, funny, and interested in a lot of things. He was there several days a week, and I al-

34

ways drove him someplace at the end of the day. Once we had lunch together at the bistro, and that was fun. He showed me a song he had written and was sending to a publisher. We're always glad to see each other.

He: He's the only straight out there. . . .

She: He's not so straight—

He: In language, I mean . . .

She: Yes. He comes from divorced parents. His father's a businessman who dips down into SB occasionally. His mother lives with an artist on the East Coast, and he's very fond of her.

He: The scene is set.

She: He took me over to show me the house where he lives with several people, and he took me next door to introduce me to his musical group. So we exchange favors, and he's been wanting to come see my castle. I feel at ease with him and enjoy being with him. I like talking to him, and it's not like talking to a feminist, where there's a skirmish going on at all times. He understands all that. . . . So, in return for his showing me his dwelling, he came out here one day. I believe it was the first time I'd shown this place to anyone. It was a beautiful day, and we took a walk down there by the pond, and we were nattering away, talking about the things we talk about. We had been discussing what he does when he's not playing in groups, and I asked, "Do you have a woman in your life?" We were walking down a trail (it's really hard to tell this), and he said, "The only woman I think about is the woman who's walking down the trail in front of me." I didn't say anything. And he said, "You're supposed to stop . . ."

He: (*Laughter*)

She: ". . . and say something pregnant." And I said, "That's only in stories or on TV," and I kept on walking. We walked on the road down below, and he said, "May I kiss you?" and I said no. And we got up to the steps out in front of this very house where we're sitting, and he said, "What I'm trying to tell you is that I'm very much attracted to you, and I'd like to sleep with you." And I said . . . I can't remember what I said. I must have indicated no. And here's why I'm telling you. I thought about why I was absolutely certain the answer was no. O, one of the things I told him was that I did this once, with a twenty-five-year-old, and I was twenty years older; now here it's happening again, and this time I'm thirty years older, and there comes a time of retirement. And I know that I'm in it. And he asked, "Have I made you very uncomfortable?" and I said, "Yes, you have." So much so that the following Thursday, which was last Thursday, on a day I knew he would be there, I didn't go to school.

He: So that's why you didn't go to school. You gave me all that song and dance. . . .

She: Is there anything in a man's life like that? Where you think, "I am a certain age, and I can't do *that* again"?

He: Yeah—it happens to me lots of times—when I think,

"No, I'm not going to write this goddamn report—I'm the president of this fuckin' company."

She: No, I mean experiences with people.

He: Yeah. I'm not going to go through any Sturm und Drang with you anymore. Either we live peacefully or not at all. I've had it.

She: The reason for my response to J. is age.

He: You're not so bloody old. . . . You've got the feelings about your mastectomy. . . . There are things you just don't want to discuss, explain, you don't want commented on. You've lived through them . . . you don't want to repeat the experience. It's boring!

Evening—restaurant
(after a movie)

She: I'll tell you about my ice-cream date with my high school sweetheart, B.

He: Where did you go on your ice-cream date?

She: The reason I haven't told you before is that it was embarrassing.

He: It was?

She: He had been calling me and asking when I would be visiting my parents. They appreciate his funny visits, and my mother loves him. He planned to visit them on Friday, and I thought I would be there too, but then I began stalling. I called him to say that I'd be quite late and not to wait for me. He visited the parents for two hours and then went to chaperone a dance. No sooner did I arrive, the telephone rang.

He: What time was it?

She: Ten o'clock. We went first to a coffee shop, and they were closing. Then we went to Jill's. He said, "Let's not go in," and I said, "You don't want anyone to see you with me, right?" He said, "You're really smart." So we sat on a bench around the corner, under a rubber tree. He says, "You're going to laugh at me. . . ." and I say, "No, I won't laugh at you." But of course he's a comical man, and once upon a time he made all of us laugh. He said that after he got married, and after his children were born, he began going into Concord to see a woman or hang out with the guys. He said, "Do you ever think about high school?" "Sure, I think about high school," I answered. "Do you ever think about sex in high school?" he asks. "Sure, I think about sex in high school. I have to think about it because that's when it all began." "Do you know why I stopped taking you out?" he wants to know. "Beats me," I tell him.

He: Do you have any idea what he's going to say?

She: No. He said that he was embarrassed and scared by the intensity of the two of us together. I was more interested in high school memories, so I said, "I don't remember too well, but I don't think we ever really did it, did we?" Remember, we're sitting on this bench, around the corner from the ice-cream parlor, thirty-nine years later.

He: No one should ever start an idle conversation with *you*. It's like pursuing a cyclone.

She: He ignored my question and said "I've been going to visit your parents, hoping they'd tell me where I could find you. . . ."

He: For thirty years!

She: I asked:, "When did you start doing that? As if I would believe you. I remember that you were an artful liar." He says, "You might as well believe me. I started visiting for that reason, but I became very fond of your mother and father."

He: What's embarrassing?

She: I had an opportunity, while we were sitting on that bench, to ask him another question I'd always wanted to ask. I said, "Remember Jim K. and his girlfriend Ruth P., and when they made love she would lose consciousness, Jim K. said, bragging. Remember you told me that? Do you remember I went out with Jim K.?" "Yes," he says. "Here's what I want to ask you," I said. "He kissed me, and I kissed back. The next week I heard from my little friend Valerie—who knew all about what folks were up to—that Jim K. did not like me because I kissed back, and I should have waited—'The shameless hussy arched her back.'" If you responded too quickly, you lost the first round.

He: What's the embarrassing part?

She: It's *all* embarrassing.

He: I think it's sort of charming.

She: It's terrible. He said:, "You weren't supposed to *like* it. I was incapable of realizing, at that time, that someone who liked it would be really good to have around." I asked:, "Are you telling me something about your marriage?"

He: (*Laughter*) You're making me laugh, and my headache is beginning to disappear.

She: I asked him why Barb and I were not invited into the girls' social clubs. Not even an initial screening. There were two good clubs and three or four we wouldn't have considered. He said, "I thought you were. I assumed. I know why Barb wasn't. No bra. Hula dancing. But no one knew anything about *you*." He has not changed at all. He looks quite the same.

He: So that was your ice-cream date. He didn't put a move on you?

She: No. In the car on the way home he said, "I don't know any goofy people except you." And I told him I was sorry.

He: Is there a story there?

She: Hush up. You have always told me of your early interest in sex. I was interested too but did not dare. I didn't want to get pregnant or have a bad reputation.

He: And boys couldn't keep their mouths shut. They were sieves. And even if they hadn't scored, they'd claim they had.

She: They counted. And they were much more interested in the girls who wouldn't than in those who would. Isn't that perverse of them?

He: It's ridiculous. I never had that fault. I was a rationalist from the very beginning. I was only interested in the girls who would.

She: I asked B. why he never introduced me to his parents. He said he was ashamed of them. Compared to mine, they were dull and stupid; they were poor and disabled.

Ride in car

He: Does it ever occur to feminist writers like Susan Griffin that the sexes are trying to attract one another, that males do as many things to make themselves sexually attractive to females as vice versa?

She: I don't think it's the making of oneself attractive to the opposite sex that they talk about. It's one sex defining what's attractive to the other and making sure, by means of power, that this is the way in which women always dress act, and then calling that the one way of behaving, and giving rewards only to the female who is dressing acting that way.

He: Do males have a wider spectrum of costume available to them than females?

She: Females aren't saying, "Males, dress in suits only. Wear ties every day to work." Women are saying, "Wear anything you want, what's comfortable, what's cool," and the men say, "Absolutely not! What would people think?"

He: So males are determining male *and* female dress. . . .

She: Yes. Something called "style" becomes dictator. And I don't believe women determine style.

He: Now, wait a minute. When women get into the business world, the world of affairs, in government, they restrict sharply the range of things they wear and become much more like males in their dress.

She: But I don't believe that's natural. When you see a sociological analysis of who succeeds and who doesn't in the business world among females, and pictures of what they were wearing when they walked in the front door, and assume all the candidates were equally qualified (say in management skills), and the survey shows high-style *Vogue* and the Mary Cunningham uniform who looks like . . .

He: . . . like a male . . .

She: No, what she looks like is a modern nun. I've seen orders where the pink shirt and the navy-blue businessy suit were the uniform. The skirt has only the slightest flare to it. It's a cross between a nun and a postwoman (mailwoman—God, our language!). Another picture shows a woman in slacks or pantsuit. Then a poll is taken, and the woman who wears a suit like Mary Cunningham, it turns out, is the woman who goes to the top. This means that at some level, if a job-seeker shows up in low-cost imported clothes (the cotton and gauzy flowing fabric), somebody in the organization will say that person is not trustworthy and shouldn't be hired. It probably happens in the initial interview. The styling gets started there. And this first interview is probably with a male. Men don't trust flair in clothes when they're thinking "work." Also, women don't necessarily like to leave their legs hanging out. It isn't always more comfortable, and men look at them and judge them: nice knees, ankles. They'd rather wear pants so that that issue doesn't come up. So you can't tell me that a woman would choose to wear . . .

He: Maybe the man doesn't either. Maybe the male is just as constrained. If a male walked in . . . in beat-up khakis he got out of the army surplus store, he wouldn't be hired either.

She: But men don't *have* to wear pantyhose in order to show that their legs are good.

He: Now, wait—a woman could walk into the interview in a pantsuit and be just as acceptable as she would in any other kind of dress.

She: This survey was conducted, and it was discovered that pantsuits were about third down the list. The Cunningham wear ranked first. The woman is there for business and also for men to look at her legs.

He: What if she has lousy legs?

She: That's too bad for her. She doesn't get hired.

He: What was the sample on this?

She: I don't know. I thought the drawing . . .

He: It just showed drawings?

She: They were pictures of women.

He: But it wasn't based on women going in and applying for a job—one woman dressed in five different ways, and send her out for interviews . . .

She: No, it was a paper survey.

He: O, ridiculous. Neither you nor I would put much credence in that. The women who come in for interviews at my company wear almost anything. Some wear dresses, some wear dressmaker suits. My goodness, I would say that on any given day, out of forty female employees, half are in some sort of slacks and half wear dresses.

She: That's after they've settled down. This survey was about when they go out to get the job, and I certainly probably would wear a dress, if I could find one.

He: There's a pretty unsexist male doing the hiring for our company, and maybe I'm blind, but I don't think anything like that goes on. I'm probably blind. But then, I'm supposed to be blind to that sort of thing. That's what I get paid to do, to make it absolutely sexless.

She: Supposing someone came in wearing the lesbian uniform—the old flannel shirt over jeans, with running shoes.

He: I wouldn't hire her. Or a gay uniform.

She: There isn't a gay uniform. Why wouldn't you hire?

He: Because there's a business uniform, and that's not it.

She: Is there a business uniform for females?

He: It's not nearly so constraining. One thing it does require—and I've just put out the word—women can wear jeans and any goddamn thing they want, but they must be clean and neat.

She: You've been putting out the word for years . . .

He: But this is true for everyone.

She: What's clean and neat?

He: Coming in with their hair straggly and looking like an unmade bed is not acceptable.

She: But that's the style now.

He: But it offends the customer and we're a service organization. If we offend the customers, they go away.

She: Do you define "clean" and "neat"?

He: No, I think "clean" and "neat" are quite adequate terms. These terms apply to everyone in the place and aren't offensive to anyone. Any male with unpressed pants or dirty shoes, or if they try to wear tennis shoes . . . males can't. Women can get away with it. But not males. They look scruffy. And it has nothing to do with their sexual preference. The marketing manager that Harry is going to sack is a female, and I think a gay man is going to get the job. And I think the San Diego office has been taken over entirely by lesbians. The manager got her cosexualists—is that what you call them?—her coreligionists in as staff.

She: Do they wear a lesbian kind of clothes?

He: They wear the business uniform. You couldn't tell they were lesbian. They dress just like the straights. It's pretty clear to everyone in the organization that sexual preference is an irrelevancy. No one gives a damn. No one looks at anyone else's behavior outside of their own.

She: You were just telling me recently that that's not true.

He: What do you mean that's not true? That's because

the lesbians became oppressive and began to push the straights around, and the straights rebelled, and the office became impossible.

She: Remember, you had a male manager who was spreading the word that one of the women was lesbian, and you were outraged that he would do that. It seems to me that this is a pretty strange tape. You led off with a discussion of how males seek to attract females, and then we wandered into a discussion of dress and abruptly shifted to sexual preference, and you have contradicted yourself at least once. You say no one in the organization is concerned with sexual preference, and yet you say the lesbians became aggressive and pushed the straights around and that the lesbians have taken over the office in San Diego.

He: Well, I mean that *top* management pays no attention to these matters until middle management gets into a muddle because of them.

She: O.

They view the ocean from the car.

She: I love to watch the changes in the ocean. . . .

He: In our new place we'll be able to see that a lot better. It would seem to me that in all of these discussions—about men, women, blacks, browns—what everyone is talking about is power, and all of these are simply symptoms of one group having power over another. The group with power can determine dress, behavior, and any goddamn thing it pleases. Now, there is the concept of a limited state so that at least the state isn't the one that's mandating injustice. So you're talking about classes. The state does not mandate behavior, language, movement, dress, sexual preference, food, or anything else.

She: The state has its grubby paw in it all along the way.

He: But at least the concept of a limited state keeps the state off the backs of the powerless somewhat, although we know, in your instance and my instance—you fighting a phony drunken reckless driving charge—the state with the dominant male had the power to exercise control. And in the case of my company, the powerful white male had the instruments of the state, and they tried to destroy me. I happen to have lived in a powerless position since 1960. And I've had to organize my life to work from the position of having no power.

She: You seem to have done pretty well.

He: I have always been confronting power from a powerless position. So, at least psychologically, I understand what it's like, and I have certain advantages—I can act like an Anglo white male so that I do have at least that much. But they see me as a traitor to my profession. There are both advantages and disadvantages.

She: You say you understand the psychology of powerlessness, but this morning you got very angry when I simply pointed out that you were using the word "man" to mean all human beings, and you went on to say that this is the English language. You were Margaret Thatcher—the colony has been taken away; we will fight to the end.

He: I just didn't think it was a legitimate way to carry on a discussion at a fairly high level of abstraction, to take a word out of the air. . . .

She: The women are taking high-level discussion and examining the words used. They are very serious about this. We don't care about high-level abstractions. We care about the language used because it has rendered us powerless and helped to make us invisible for thousands of years. If you don't like it, I'm afraid you're in for a lot more of it.

He: I'm willing to use a synonym. When I'm discussing philosophy . . .

She: No man has ever wanted a tampering with the language when he's proclaiming Truth.

He: You just tell me the words you want me to use so that we get away from the semantics.

She: "Humankind." "Humanity."

He: "Humanity" is just as bad. You're going to have to invent . . .

She: No, I can't invent.

He: Mathematicians invent words.

She: For the last ten years feminists have been working hard making "man" a nervous word in one's mouth. The word "culture" has been worked over.

He: How about wo*man*? Or fe*male*?

She: You are described in so many books. You are being snide. One of the techniques is to belittle and show how funny it all is.

He: Language is very tricky.

She: And one of the tricks that's played is to totally obscure the female in history. The language obscures an already shadowy person.

He: Culture, it seems to me, is nonsexist in the sense that I can't see whether it's feminine or masculine.

She: But it's always connected with man's doings. The culture of man, the history of man. Charlotte Gilman had a suggestion that we always put the men in when they want to be there rather than finding a word which includes women. For instance, British males sailed off to reclaim the Falklands from the Argentine males and sank a sub "manned" by Argentine males and saved a few men and lost several hundred Argentine males.

He: Hmm. Who's Charlotte Gilman?

She: No one.

He: Let me come back to the subject of language. What do the Spanish, the Germans, the French, the Italians do about the fact that the word has a gender?

She: They have many neuter words, abstract words. In Spanish, "mankind" is "la humanidad"—that is, a feminine noun, and if you go on to say, "Man solves his problems . . ." in Spanish one says, "Man(kind) solves *its* problems"—so that at least the Spanish language is more graceful, less taunting and brutal. There is "la luna" and "el sol," which probably goes way back to myth. We'll have to check with Angelo.

He: Let me ask you this. Do you really want to desex the language? Couldn't we look at sexual differences in the same way we look at socialism versus a free-market society? Most of the criticism that has been leveled against socialist economies that the state becomes an oppressive enforcer of the least common denominator and everything gets a little grayer and grayer and the differences disappear—innovation, creativity, and adventure. By contrast, the free-market society leads to exploitation by the strong, and our sense of equity, whether it's a natural sense or not, cries out that we must regulate the market. But if you regulated the market completely, society would become so dull that why bother anyway.

She: Do you know what you're doing right now, in feminist terms?

He: What?

She: Giving a lecture.

He: Well, I might be giving a lecture, but the point is . . .

She: . . . and the women would stop right there and say, "We are having a discussion; we are not listening to a lecture."

He: I've finished with the lecture.

She: We aren't any farther along on the question of desexing the language.

He: Do you really want to desex the language?

She: I managed to live until I was into my fifties without ever noticing that "mankind" said "*man*kind" and didn't include me. Every time I read "human," I thought male and female. "Mankind" meant men, women, and children. Every time I thought "brotherhood," I assumed sisters too.

He: So did I.

She: In my fifties I received a confusing shock.

He: You found out what "bruderschaft" really meant?

She: Many of the writers I've been reading were sensitized to it earlier and felt damaged by it. I didn't even notice.... If one does not feel limited by the terms used, it doesn't matter what words are used—"man," "woman," or "dolphin." I felt myself to be a part of it. However, if one grows up thinking it peculiar that "his" means everybody's and "hers" does not, one acquires scars. And now that attention has been called to this peculiarity of the English language, the attention may lapse, as it did in the '20s....

He: I hope not because I don't like unliberated women. And I don't like unliberated blacks or unliberated Chicanos.

She: If the consciousness of sex bias in the language continues to persist, we are going to have to try to change the language. And I hope that makes the women feel better so that they can get back to allowing language to have consensual meanings. It's now very hard to talk.

He: I grew up feeling much the same way you did—it was brotherhood, sisterhood, childrenhood, everybodyhood—so why can't the two of us make a secret pact that I'm not a sexist, you're not a sexist? There's no use having a private war going on, that there will be an area of pain between the two of us, and we can watch the war and you can point out the nature of my language, but you don't have to beat me up about it. We can't do that?

She: I won't say we can't, but it will be difficult. Although for fifty years I've lived peacefully with the language, now there's a current that goes through me because I've received from my feminist culture some knowledge and some preparation for listening that I'd never received before. So I can't listen in the same way.

He: I don't mind your pointing it out to me. It doesn't bother me in the slightest.

She: We cannot use the language as it's been used before. We have to give some sign that we're aware, or that she is aware that the words she's using with this man are words which have been discussed and are tainted.

He: That you're using the language of slavery, but you're doing it knowingly. . . .

She: If I can, I'll use the language of slavery. If it offends me, I'll back off. Which leads me to ask, what is happening when a woman says to a man, "Don't use that word"? What we're talking about is immediately forgotten, and the men begin to defend *their* language. *The* English language.

He: It's just as if you were forcing me to speak Spanish! At some point I say, "I don't care if I never learn Spanish! I'm going to say what's on my mind!" And that's why I've never been able to learn any language. Shakespeare, from everything I've read, was androgynous.

She: Yes, he could move around as man or woman; his pronouns were agile. And he had few humble females.

He: Except for Ophelia, they're strong, tough ladies.

She: Desdemona.

He: Let's get back to my minilecture, which I don't think of as a lecture. I think it's making a precise point in a historical, philosophical context. Are feminists really sure they want to desex the language and have as few differences as they would seem to want? Or are they going to find an enormous variety, an intention that is exciting—are they going to lose those things?

She: I don't have another word for "mankind." I would like there to be "actor" and "actress." I believe the feminists want "poet" to mean both female and male. I wish our language had a feminine and a masculine. I like the difference residing in "poet" and "poetess." It interests me to know what kind of body is making the pictures. "Amiga" is a female friend. It means something different from "amigo" and our word "friend."

He: Your friend Sally suggests, states, that heterosexual sex is the exception, the unnatural, and that homosexual society is the natural order of things. She uses tortured logic.

She: Does she arrive at this position from her body or from logic?

He: From logic. It's bad logic and scholarship. The logic is that originally in the family, and from nurturing between the mother and child, a primary bond is established for both men and women with the mother, the female.

She: I would say that there's a big difference between bonding with your mother, because of one's physical closeness to her, and sleeping with her. Never did I have a sexual fantasy about my mother. I didn't even want to hug her because of her corsets. Nor did I want to sleep with my father. I liked dogs and soft cats, horses.

He: You had a tendency toward bestiality. . . .

She: I liked things that were soft and wouldn't hurt me. Sunshine, flowers. My father could rip me apart. So could my mother. Best to stay away from them.

He: Right!

She: Where does that leave us?

He: What I think is rather interesting is the ability to take these arguments to their logical and, as far as I can see, totally absurd conclusions.

She: Yes.

He: One of the things which is going to be an interesting

problem for you is how you're going to sequence these conversations. You'll have to thematically break them down. . . .

She: Not necessarily . . .

He: They have a sort of organic dialectic?

She: It's like Tinker Bell coming into Peter Pan's life over and over again—just when he thinks he's got things going well with the Darling family, then Tinker Bell comes in with her jealousy. The irritation which is now current between men and women asserts itself in the most idyllic circumstances and causes conversations to begin in one place and dart off into strange, dangerous canyons. So I don't know that I want to theme the book.

He: You could begin with an essay which would refer to conversations so that you could say what you think they all add up to. Then the conversations could stand on their own.

She: I'm not sure I'd like to summarize and decide what the conversations "say."

He: I see. Don't you want to become a famous feminist theorist?

She: No.

He: You don't want to be just a passive participant in a series of conversations, do you?

She: Yes, I do. I think Sally should ask herself whether her theories, as set forth by Adrienne Rich, are like the river: whether they flow or are tortured damned viaducts, and whether they would ever have produced her very beauti-

ful child, my friend Samual. Do her theories have any relation to nature?

Furthermore, I'm tired of hearing what Tillie Olsen says
or said. She's the spokeswoman for a generation, and I don't
think she deserves it.

Dinner

He: When I really get a hit, I'm going to bring you one, two, three strands of pearls.

She: You know I hardly ever get dressed up. I wouldn't know what to wear them with. So you took the article over to your old friend Angelo . . .

He: . . . and it led to all sorts of revelations. The article states that heterosexual sex is unnatural, that the true order of things is sex between lesbians because of the early bond between mothers and daughters. And what males do, I don't know. I guess they just wander around in the ozone.

She: They're free agents until they're needed.

He: And then I suppose they ejaculate into a spoon or something. I found Angelo startlingly favorable toward feminists and he felt that it was receding. I didn't feel that way. I see it as gaining strength. I might be wrong. I've wasted many years of my life in movements that I thought were gaining strength when they were plateaued. Wouldn't this sort of thing really act as a corrosive on society? And he said, "You can forget it—never, ever will feminism, or lesbianism, have an effect on that society." And I said, "Well, you can't be sure," and he said again that his perception is that feminism is receding, that it had to do with the '60s and the advances made by minorities. Now ERA has gone down the tubes. Feminism has reached its apogee and is heading the other way. And I said, "If that is so, it's because they don't organize. However they perceive they should organize, they don't structure themselves and have decision-making units which can make a decision." And he said, "O, no, that's not what feminism is all about. It would be a denial of the whole thing. Feminism is an attempt to construct society on matriarchal relationships in which they spend enormous amounts of time reaching consensus." He said it's amazing how tolerant they are with one another in these discussions. He said they will hear someone out and they never interrupt, and they're very protective of the sisters who might not be very cogent. He said that although this means that many of their decisions are compromises, that the strength of the groups is that when they finally agree, almost everyone is willing at that point to act. But they don't want to build very large organizations. They fear size and want to keep the smaller units. Within those smaller units they are even more powerfully old-girl than men are old-boy. They have knee-jerk responses to the requests of the sisters.

She: I'm finding their knee-jerk responses to the poets in this area very annoying. There are certain poets they worship—Rich, Griffin.

He: Agreed.

She: Yes. To another subject. Pornography. Susan Griffin says that the pornographers act like liberals and claim they are providing a service. If there weren't pornographic films and magazines, think of what men would have to do! This is, of course, hogwash. In countries where pornography is relatively free, the incidence of rape has not decreased. Singleton, the nut who cut off that fifteen-year-old's arms, pleaded with the judge that he had read of terrible crimes and that this girl was walking around alone, was not dressed properly, and she made overtures toward him. What was he to do?

He: Cut her arms off, of course. That was his only recourse. What did he get?

She: Fourteen years for rape, sodomy, oral copulation, kidnapping, mayhem, and attempted murder.

He: Pleaded with the judge for clemency?

She: He was saying that she was *there*, and that was provocative.

He: He probably wouldn't have gotten so much time if he'd kept his mouth shut.

She: He might have killed her. He left her for dead, bleeding from stumps.

He: But he had a history of sex crimes, didn't he?

She: I don't believe so. He was a drunk who beat his daughter. That was one of the times that my children accused me of being morbid in following the case. But my daughter had just returned from having hitchhiked with a friend, and I was frightened.

THEO'S FOR DINNER

She: Here's something that interests me. What has been the effect of the feminist movement on you?

He: Boy, that's a global question.

She: But we've often talked around it.

He: My generalization would be deleterious. Certainly it's not something I enjoy, and I feel that I've been punished for others' sins. I find a bumper sticker such as "Women need men like fish need bicycles" to be crude, untrue, strident, and . . . stupid.

She: Not a bit funny?

He: I don't think that there's any consistent ideology. I think the movement's sadly lacking in intellectual distinction. I wish it were otherwise, but that's the way I feel.

She: What sort of intellectual distinction?

He: I'd like to see it be at least as good as Freudianism, which I think has been pretty bad. Primarily, it has caused trouble with *you*. It's confused you and caused you to be strident and to behave in ways that you don't really want to behave. You felt it was incumbent upon you for some reason—why, God knows.

She: Do you feel you've learned anything from it?

He: Yeah, to keep my mouth shut.

She: I haven't noticed you keeping your mouth shut.

He: To be guarded in my conversation, particularly with you.

She: You learned that long before the movement.

He: I suppose it has all the emotions of the black movement and "viva la raza." I'm not saying it isn't justified. I think women have been pushed around for a long time. But for a long time they were coconspirators, and presumably they thought they were getting a good deal, so if any group ever sold out themselves, it's the females. And then circumstances changed, society changed, and they ended up on the short end of the stick.

She: What circumstances changed?

He: O, the changing nature of labor, the decline of the nuclear family, the fact that housewifery ceased to be a viable occupation. During the period when it was a viable occupation they gave up labor in the fields and the factory for the security and ease of the home. They also lost economic rights they previously had—rights to jobs.

She: What century is this?

He: Remember Tess of the d'Urbervilles—they had as much right to agricultural labor as anybody. And then there's the question—society has always had to figure out what in hell to do about the labor involved in childbearing. It's not an easy activity to socialize in such a way that it's just. You start out with death in childbirth. In the nineteenth-century graveyards, most of the gravestones are women.

She: Or tiny children.

He: That isn't very fair! It's like Tennyson's statement about nature . . . so solicitous of the species, so indifferent to the individual! *You* would have died in childbirth, that first time, had you lived in the nineteenth century.

She: Can you remember how it was different before women were strident?

He: Romance was possible. There was mystery.

She: You and I can slip in and out of romance when we have a mind to.

He: We haven't done it very often very recently.

She: What is there about romance that is in opposition to feminism?

He: I don't know. I think of my job, creating a company, as very romantic. And I don't worry about poverty and inequity. I don't puzzle my little head on whether it's ultimately good. I just decide, well, it isn't going to put me in jail. It's probably doing somebody some good. It isn't brain surgery. I don't like all the heavy burden that comes with management. In other words, when Socrates said the unexamined life is not worth living, I'd say the corollary is true—the examined life is not worth living. It becomes a ruddy goddamn bore.

She: So you find feminism boring.

He: Yes, pretty boring. For instance, I haven't seen very many comedies about it. Feminism has got to come to terms with heterosexuality. I don't find homosexuality terribly attractive. It is very dangerous.

She: Why are you talking about homosexuality?

He: Because you asked me about the feminist movement. A big strand of the feminist movement is lesbian.

She: They're not particularly promiscuous.

He: I didn't say they were, but if lesbianism is good for females, its counterpart must be good for males as well. And I don't think it is.

She: Perhaps it's good for females but not for males.

He: Well, if you're going to argue that homosexuality is a viable lifestyle, then presumably it must be viable for males and females—or is it only viable for half the human race?

She: Lesbianism is often a political statement, and I don't think men loving men is. What would it be a statement about?

He: I find political statements having to do with sexuality puzzling.

She: I do too. The anger is very deep.

He: The anger of male homosexuals is deep against heterosexual men and women. Anita Bryant is more a symbol of oppression against the homosexual community than any male might have been. Now, let me ask you, what is your feeling toward the feminist movement now that you've been observing it closely for three years?

She: I don't read *Ms.* anymore. I'm tired of the old tracks they dig. I'm not sure anymore what a feminist point of view is, or exactly why there's a necessity for one.

He: You've been giving Ellen Bass's book a critical reading. Is it a feminist book?

She: I would call it a lesbian book, and this is for me a new category I've been reluctant to admit. It's stifling. There is criticism of the husband she has just left, but it is not really a female-versus-male book. They weren't happy together, and she is happy with her female lover. With marked emphasis on sex, sense of humor, and the child. No, it's not a feminist book. Her complaints about her husband could just as well apply to a female who was living with her. He didn't help with the baby, but he did have scoliosis, and it was painful to lift. Not helping with the baby is a feminist cry, trite, but this particular husband had his reasons. The novella centers around the people in her environment who have physical pain. Her lover is also in pain. It's a little book about living around people who hurt, but what makes it a lesbian book is the explicit sex. This doesn't seem fair, but that's the way I feel.

He: Well, you don't like my pain when I drag myself through the door.

She probably just has a very low tolerance for someone else's pain.

She: Curious, because she's in pain too.

He: All writers are in pain. They're pretty self-centered. They find it very difficult to reach out to other people. I've read quite a bit about writers, and I think I could be writhing on the floor about to die, and they would just as soon ignore it.

She: I think that's grossly unfair.

He: Tolstoy would have done the same thing. Hemingway. I think what you did is wear out your nurture part with those kids. For instance, it's impossible for you to compose a quarrel. . . .

She: Here we go . . .

He: Now, wait a minute. I'm not saying that's bad. I admire it.

She: Lying in bed last night, I couldn't sleep but was quite content to lie beside you, and I kept thinking of my own attitudes toward pain. I have a very low pain threshold, as you know, and I can remember that one of my earliest memories of irritation with my mother was her emphasis on *my* pain. Part of her nurturing was to make a big thing of every hurt, illness, wound of mine. She also celebrated her own. My father, on the other hand, rarely hurt except for his two illnesses, kidney stones and gout. When he had either of these very literary ailments, he went to pieces. He cried, moaned, talked of nothing else. I was very small when I first began to think of my two parents as needing pain. I couldn't figure out why but knew it was so. He would go all out, and she would nurture all out, and I remember being punished for behaving normally during these bouts. I wasn't supposed to be cheerful or play jacks. To her dying day, she wanted pain

66

to nurture—my pain, what ached, who else had symptoms. It might get worse; you'll die of it. She was a pain lover. You see an indifference to pain in me, and part is reaction. I didn't want to live that way. On the other hand, I have three children, and from the beginning of their lives their attitude toward pain was different. If one of the girls banged her finger, it was cry, cry, cry, blame someone else. With him, even with his auto accident, he didn't complain that he hurt. A genetic difference? Male female?

He: Back to feminism. It seems to me that it's dealt as harshly with you as it has with me.

She: I was unbalanced to begin with, and it created a worse imbalance. Which you have seen.

He: Boy, have I! What feminism did to you was almost rob you of your sexuality.

She: And now?

He: I said almost.

She: It has invaded all of us; it's everywhere. Perhaps not in Japan, which you've recently visited.

He: No, not over there.

She: There are a number of Japanese female novelists who speak strongly.

He: Not in the popular press. What gets me is that feminism gave you sort of a mechanical view of sex in which you decided that there were certain things which were not supposed to give pleasure.

She: I was aware long before feminism. I never before had a podium from which I could announce my irritation that the penis was absolute king. I don't think one has to be a feminist to find this unsatisfactory. It's a fact of life, and when one lives with a man who wishes to express himself in bed, he does it again and again and again, and nothing much happens to the woman. This is being written about.

He: It only takes a tiny bit of assertiveness on the female side to right that imbalance.

She: That's not true. Most men, though they be sensitive, want to call all the shots. They don't want to learn anything. They just want to do it and hope, even pray, that what they do is pleasurably received. Some as quickly as possible, others five times a night.

He: I've begged you to educate me, and you've found that very difficult. And you won't just say, "Hey, now, here's what I want you to do."

She: That's mechanical.

He: Mechanical-shemanical.

She: I've talked to you, and you don't change. Much.

He: The only reason I don't change is that I don't understand what you're telling me.

She: Difficult to tell you anything regarding changing your behavior. Last night, on another subject, you said, "That's the way I am. I will not change." When the feminist says, "Look, you don't do it right," they're saying they want some enjoyment too. But it seems to me now that men and women in bed are both ideally designed for each other *and* are different species trying to cross over. Last night, in the midst of my wakefulness, I wondered what the count would be if you totaled it all up. If occasionally I have four or five orgasms in one evening, and every night you have one or two, perhaps in the great design we come out even.

He: I never thought of that.

She: Perhaps this arrangement, the spacing, has a biological defense.

He: Different cycles may protect babies. I've never counted. I never think about it. I just enjoy it so much I just assume it's that pleasurable for you.

She: But it isn't. This is what women want to say, and they want to say it in every possible way they can think of to say it. Men make war, language, don't listen. All connected.

He: But I enjoy giving you pleasure so much when you have it that I don't understand why you don't feel the same toward me.

She: I do—when I get started. It's in the nature of the act that *you're* ready from the beginning.

He: It puzzles me that you don't want me to have pleasure—really *puzzles* me!

She: I do, up to a certain point.

He: Up to what point? I use that term advisedly.

She: I feel locked into a life balance similar to that with

ex-husband. He could go on and on, and the question he never asked, and most men don't—no, he did ask the question because he came out of the Berkeley milieu of the late '40s, where women were expected to be just as actively in pursuit of pleasure as the men. They were great lovers if they responded and were "frigid" if they didn't.

He: So C. expected you to react and enjoy, and then he laid some Freudian analysis on the wedding bed.

She: Yes, he expected me to measure up to his sexuality, and sometimes I have thought that there is a sense in which all of feminism is a fury at being asked to measure up to, conform to, male sexuality. It comes up again and again in what they write. When I believe they're talking about politics or rights, back they hop to this prior resentment. In experimenting with the Freudian sexual revolution, it almost seems as though women tried to match their pleasure to that of men, tried to explain, tried to wriggle and writhe and make it happen, and when they had amassed a pile of disappointment, they simply exploded and began saying to the men, "I'm going to sleep with women, I'm going to kill you, I'm going to make your marriages rot, I'm going to run away from you and join the sisters, I'm not going to put up with what's been going on between men and women from the beginning of time." I think that's why they seem so unpleasant and strident when talking about quite minor issues. It's almost a massive, furious jealousy of the constant male pleasure.

He: But I don't feel myself guilty of these things. I've never resisted being introduced into the mysteries.

She: I don't know how you could have paid attention if you were urged on by your body to mount a woman five times a day. You couldn't have had time to pause.

He: I don't think that's true.

She: Did they all rise up and say, "Bravo"?

He: I'm not saying that any of them did, but I certainly would never have resisted instruction. I'd have thought, "O, man, I'm learning something new. Something that will serve me in good stead in times to come."

She: Learning from one to apply to others? Plowing a field of women. Any woman could have seen your agenda . . . and declined. You make it sound like you were attending a sex college, which no doubt you were.

He: I would like to know why you and other women were so reluctant to instruct men.

She: I've just given you a few of the reasons. I can think of no female who regards coupling or sex as a training program for future events. They do not think of their sexuality in that way. They may learn a great deal about their bodies by loving other women, and welcome it, but it's not a training program. And you don't stand still long enough. You say, "Just let me put it in." At first you were rather sweetly compliant and cooperative when I explained, but then you began to say that it inhibited you to have to prepare me.

He: Well, that's the advantage of anointing yourself.

She: Instructing the male—how silly. We're two different species and are *meant* to be mismatched.

He: Now, wait a minute—you know as well as I do that if you're anointed with massage oil so that there is no trauma to entry, I can be in and out of you, I can be stroking you, and I can spin it out for as long as you want.

She: Speaking purely personally, and not about women in general, about which I know nothing, you just spend too much time thinking about sex. It's not that important to me.

He: I don't think about it if you don't resist.

She: Last night we had a great night, and I think, "O, lawsy, now he'll be all revved up and maybe tonight is a different night altogether." Six orgasms is not a program for me. Maybe one night, and then perhaps not for two weeks.

He: I see.

She: And men won't put up with it. They say every night, every night, and then they go out and make companies and do international relations. With me it's mood and circumstance and the real romance . . .

He: What in hell is the real romance?

She: Between a man and a woman.

He: I could be simpleminded and say, what else is there?

She: You were talking earlier about the romance of business . . .

He: It's every day!

She: And it's every day with sex too. How about your business friend D.? Does he do without because of traveling 90 percent of the time?

He: Didn't I tell you the other day he said, "God, it's great to be in a sexy business!" (*Much laughter*)

She: The more you tell me about him, the more obnoxious he sounds. I hope his wife has a marvelous lover. I hope she's had one for twenty years. Maybe two or three. A place away from her house so that when he bops in . . .

He: He always gives plenty of notice. It would be almost impossible for him to arrive unexpected. There's a stream of telexes preceding his [arrival].

She: She should pull the plug.

He: So long as she has a halfway decent relationship with his secretary, she has, at the minimum, twelve hours' notice.

She: I hope she sees people who are whole. People like P. are berserk. He's number eight or nine on your list of men you admire. You have a long list, and there's never been a woman among them. I haven't met very many of them. I did meet P. He's a total dunce. Not a human being. I haven't met the other ones.

He: You've been blessed.

She: These long affairs, sometimes for several years, and you tell me so-and-so has said to you and isn't that outrageous, clever, etc. Each time I think, "A woman wouldn't like that clever saying, or think him intelligent." . . . A particular kind of man intrigues you. The doer, the deal-maker, the manipulator, the builder. The kind who eliminates women from meaningful roles in his life.

In graduate school, true friends were those you played poker with, made jokes with, caroused with. These long-term admirations are affairs. They last a long time. And if I say, "I really think such and such a woman is an interesting and smart female," you say, "I don't have intellectual love affairs anymore." Right now P. is our beau ideal. You spend days and days with him, watch the way he acts, the way he dresses.

He: I'm trying to learn everything he knows.

She: It's more than that. It's an attraction.

He: O, yes. Fascination. How did he do it? How did he get all that together?

She: And since you've been with P. you've become much more macho.

He: More?

She: It waxes and wanes. You see over there in the orient an absolutely clear field of women in their twenties. They're decorative and receiving and silent.

He: They swish when they walk by. You can hear their skirts.

She: They're minted, designed, trained to please men. This is about as far away as you can get from American feminism. You come back from the orient, and here I am.

He: Like a rock in the middle of the road. A pothole.

(*Both laugh.*)

She: Part of the general decay, corruption, and general obtuseness of SB.

He: A pothole is a place where the road is eroding away in the middle on out to the sides.

She: I read many books—from the machos, the South American authors, and lately a Mishima book he wrote just before he died, from the Japanese culture. A strange, gross report on how he prepared himself to commit suicide. He had to build his body and muscles with sun and steel in order to be in perfect condition for death. The South American writers seldom see themselves apart from their macho, Catholic heritage . . . it's a rich compote.

He: There is a great difference between South American machismo and P.

She: In a continuum of machismo, one goes from the South American to the American, which in the strictest sense of the word is homosexual. It is a life without women.

He: Let me put it this way. He is an Anglo macho who is concerned with deals. I have never seen him look at a female. He isn't interested in making out. He doesn't want a mistress. That would just be a bother. He is dedicated to meeting his responsibilities.

She: The last tape, I became more and more inarticulate, stupider, fuzzier in speech, and you, the more you drank, the words rolled more easily and freely off your tongue.

He: I'm an experienced, professional drinker.

She: But I am, even without wine, disadvantaged when talking about things I know nothing about, like business.

He: Listen, if you could learn anything about business by reading magazines, then everyone in the goddamn country would be a very bright businessman. I read those magazines, but they have almost no application. I don't read about management. I read about the economy. I read to find out where is the opening in the market, what could I produce that would sell. But as for management, I make it up as I go along.

She: Is there anything else you'd like to say about men and women?

He: I'm before the court. "Is there anything you'd like to say before I sentence you?"

She: We've said very little about children on the tapes. Nothing about the other woman in Seattle.

He: You won't let me talk about that.

She: I would let you, but I don't want it in the book. Censorship. It would require development by you, and I don't think I could hear that speech again without vomiting.

He: Do I laugh a lot in the tapes? (*Laughter*) What do you put down? "Chuckle"? One thing . . . you said the other day . . . or someone was . . . about the woman who married three strong, silent men . . . she had this girlish view that they were really the most desirable. . . .

She: Not I . . . some other person.

He: It was probably M. And after the third one, she said the reason they're silent is that they have nothing to say. They are dull.

She: Well, Lindbergh wasn't dull. With most men, it isn't that they talk too much, it's *what* they say and the way they say it which turns their talk into mosquito bombardment. Lindbergh was not dull, and he was strong and silent. A man of few, well-chosen words. Still, he should probably have talked less.

He: I'm sure there are exceptions. Anyway, this woman said there is a certain minimum amount of conversation that is necessary to keep any relationship going, whether it be male-male, male-female. There's a bare minimum, and if a person can't sustain that as time goes on, I suspect that connection dies. That movie we saw the other night—*Chilly Scenes of Winter*—it occurred to me that probably most of the people I know, male and female, bore me. I would imagine that male and female relationships among that mass of humanity that I find pretty dull, are dull. The subjects, the content—and I perceive they wouldn't be of much interest to me whether they were macho males or nonmacho—the content would be dull no matter what the prevailing ideology is.

She: Most people bore me too, but I am interested in how men and women work it out, in hearing women talk about their men and vice versa, up to a point.

He: That movie—you found it interesting. I found it excruciatingly dull.

She: O, come, now. You sat there, you chuckled, your eyes were bright, you were listening.

He: Well, he had an interesting face.

She: But the people who interest you are those who can help you in your business . . . and your son . . . and occasionally me. You've already decided that you're very bored with anything that goes on between men and women in general, and you couldn't read the novel *Chilly Scenes of Winter* or any of Ann Beattie's other books.

He: I'd go stark, raving crazy.

She: The tapestry doesn't interest you. Beattie isn't one of my favorites, but I think I'd rather read about her characters than about Rabbit.

He: I'd have trouble with Updike, as you describe him, too.

She: Then there's a character in *The Water-Method Man*, by John Irving, who is such a losing, flailing, nonacting resident of earth, you would be incapable of turning the pages. And I had trouble. But I think I keep turning because I'm interested in John Irving. Which reminds me. Did you know that Nabokov said, "I think like a genius. I write like an intelligent artist," or something along those lines, "and I speak like a child." He couldn't talk well.

He: I obviously like to read about people. Tolstoy, Dostoyevsky. Emma wasn't heroic. Hester Prynne is heroic. I got through *The Scarlet Letter* because it's a classic. Terribly written book.

She: It's a classic because it deals with a subject which bothered his century in a nice gothic way. It's very difficult to read. Styles change.

He: No one ever spoke that way.

She: But people speak in ways today which make your eyes glaze . . . your friend M.'s J., when she talks of mundane things, the stuff most young women are interested in.

He: She's one of the most boring women I've ever spent five minutes with.

She: And yet my son has spent enjoyable time with her.

He: He's an artist. He's interested in people. They're raw material. She's raw material for him. But not for me.

She: I find it just as boring when people have their minds on business.

He: No reason why you shouldn't feel that way. Very understandable. But I'm not the only one who finds J. dull. M. does too.

She: That's his fault. There's something askew in a man of his powers who goes on and on with a woman who bores him.

He: I didn't pursue it.

She: It seems to me that he should quit futzing around and, if the answer is no, should tell her so and depart. That's what's dumb.

He: She is. I told you. A bore.

She: I didn't say *she's* dumb; I said the whole thing is dumb, stuff of stagnant realism stories and novels. He goes every night to her bed, but he hasn't committed himself. Dumb.

He: Why, when there are so many boring men and women in this world, should I be concerned with male-female relationships? Maybe what we've been talking about is how to survive in a relatively interesting combination. I don't know how you regard me, but I find you . . . probably of all the women I've ever met, you have the most interesting mind.

She: Not apparent on these tapes, perhaps. Flattery.

He: Not flattery. The only times you bore me are when you get into these set pieces when you say the world should be structured in a particular way, and if it isn't structured that way it's irrelevant, grotesque. There's one thing that bothers me about you.

She: Only one?

He: Of this nature. You are totally tolerant of gross behavior, of dull people, undull people, historical people, yet you will be the most narrow bourgeois on occasion.

She: I'll tell you something about both you and your son. Something which skyrockets me into fury. The smile on the face of the superior being amongst fools.

He: I don't think I sit there and smile.

She: You do. At all the foolish people who try to come up

with answers, all muddled and muggy. Maybe because you believe you have answers or believe that there are no answers. . . .

He: What's this got to do with your bourgeois rigidity? Juxtaposed against your acceptance of damn near anything that rolls down the pike? Not only acceptance, but you can describe it with great interest and apparent approval. Nothing is unacceptable. In literary terms, you're the most tolerant person I've ever met.

She: You posture. The others, of whom I'm tolerant, do not.

He: In fact, as long as a person doesn't try to make contact with you and isn't the trailside murderer, and you don't know the person, you're completely tolerant of everyone!

She: We're not naming names, but sometimes I'm interested. You put people into boxes and categories, and that doesn't work well for me. I'd like to tell you about Phil.

He: Yes. Phil.

She: You have not ever talked with Phil even though he's worked for you. That would have seemed a waste of time to you. He talks and thinks too slowly, too laid back. I never know what's going to come out of his mouth. But you wouldn't wait to find out. Years, three years, I've seen him every day at work, and today I admired a shirt he was wearing which had embroidered butterflies. I asked who embroidered it. He said a friend. I said she must have loved him a lot. Yeah, a lot. Was it a long time ago? "Ten years ago she embroidered it. She's the mother of punk Julie. Matter of fact, I was with her last night." Then he pauses and says, "Punk Julie, she's just as beautiful punk as she was when she was a little tiny girl." So I said, "That's what you say about Julie's younger sister too, and I know you sometimes spend the night at their mother's house, and I'd like to ask you . . . do you fall in love with girls that young (fourteen)?" He says, "O, man, do I!" He says he organizes his life so that he will continue to watch them grow until they're ripe. Then what? "I'll have to wait another year." Knowing someone like Phil takes time and sympathy. He really likes the mothers, and he likes to be part of the training and upbringing of the girls, and eventually . . . ?

He: Does he start something?

She: Probably.

He: Does the mother mind?

She: I don't know. Probably not. Now who's being bourgeois?

He: It's illegal. You should turn him in. People in the neighborhood wanted to jail the guy who was doing it with boys.

She: Phil himself wants that guy to go to jail and get killed. He has no tolerance for him. He says he's pulling his power on helpless young boys. I don't agree with his solution.

He: How about young girls?

She: Phil doesn't have any power. He just lies back. He's

an artist who enjoys beauty. He plays Bach on the flute and watches the human female emerge, like a butterfly. Obviously they like it. They flee to him when their mothers want them to do the dishes. Phil watches them; I watch Phil. It's a slow process. While you talk about international business and the center of the universe, the city in the head, and all the world cities, I watch Phil, and others. Sometimes I wonder how you can spend your time with a woman who dwells on such unimportant matters.

He: They aren't unimportant. Now, let me just get around to the fact that you accuse me of using people. *You* use people. Your interest and your tolerance lie in the fact that the more bizarre the behavior, the more valuable they are.

She: That's not using people the way you use them.

He: Yes, it is.

She: We're verging on a discussion I don't want to get into.

He: Are you pulling your bourgeois rank on me again?

She: I serve you in only one way, and you can't use me for public goals. I can't further your major objectives, and therefore you can't manipulate me.

He: That's balderdash. Everyone needs relaxation. You amuse me. You can be charming, outrageous, witty. . . .

She: There's a world of women out there. . . .

He: I've met a lot of women, and there aren't very many who are charming.

She: It's dry out there? I would think M could find someone a little more . . .

He: M wants someone boring. He's narcissistic. Even more than I am. He's not interested in anyone but himself.

She: If I were M., I would be terrified that J.'s awkward gifts would make inroads on my private pursuits and somehow turn them to ash . . . to muddle the images into muck.

He: Well, he tells me that she sometimes lies in bed and cries for many hours.

She: Because life is so unfair . . . things don't line up right or turn out?

He: And he says, "It infuriates me! I can't get anything done!"

She: I know how he feels. And I do the same.

He: Well, I don't stay around for an hour's crying. But she's in *his* bed, so therefore she gets to cry.

She: Sometimes you stay around.

He: Only long enough to stanch the tears and figure out how I can get out.

She: You pretend to be so tough.

He: Yes, you amuse me. You lovingly place your sheath over me.

She: Anyone can do that. We're all equipped.

He: I know, but I happen to like yours . . . the temperature. . . .

She: Are there some which are freezing cold, red hot?

He: I can't explain it . . . tee-hee-tee-hee . . . you laugh.

Anyway, I think yours is just as unexamined a life as mine. You claim to have examined it. . . .

She: No, I don't. I do enough of that when I work. Quite enough. But as to whether or not this is the ethical thing, whether I should be doing it, whether it's the right man I'm with, or should I be with any man, I don't spend time on that. I go like the turtle, the path of least resistance.

He: Me too.

She: Ha! More like the opposite.

He: But you still haven't made any response to my observation that you're very tolerant to historical and fictional figures but, say with your daughter, you . . .

She: Why do you keep mentioning what you call my intolerance of my daughter? It doesn't *matter* that she's my daughter. I don't have the notion you have, to hang on to the blood link and soar into their future with my offspring. She and I have agreed to avoid each other at the present time. We don't mesh with each other. Everything I say to her starts her emotions boiling. She will change, and maybe I'll be in her life, and maybe I won't. I can't force it. You say I'm intolerant of you and I'm intolerant of my daughter, but I'm not.

He: You're indifferent to your daughter.

She: Not so.

He: Well, what are you to your daughter?

She: Right now I'm in a period of noncommunication. She comes to me and says she wants a $25,000 wedding because it's traditional and says further that I should pay for it in order to prove to her that I love her. My response is to back off and wait for the next news. If your son told you that, and you didn't have $25,000, what would you say?

He: I'd suggest a $10 wedding. Every wedding I've ever had has cost $10.

She: My first one was . . .

He: . . . big and expensive . . .

She: Not big . . . many flowers, at my home.

He: I don't think that I'm that dull, and furthermore, I don't think the fact that there's an international city in my brain and that I want to learn all its suburbs is of any more importance than P. or Julie the punker. I've told you before that I really agree with the existentialists that life is absurd. The only thing that gives it importance is my interest in it. You're interested in punk; I'm interested in the world city. I would bore A. to death, and she would bore me to death in seconds.

She: Your son doesn't, and he's just as far out.

He: I don't think you understand that I'm a teacher, and whether he's conning me or not, he's led me to believe that he wants to learn what I know and he's willing to do an apprenticeship.

WILLOWS RESTAURANT, HONOLULU
(LAST NIGHT OF TRIP)

He: I want to have a conversation about the feminine mystique because I am not persuaded that males are the main source of female problems. I've watched you, in the presence of males who are urging you to stand on your own two feet, offering you help to do it—myself in particular—and a violent rejection, of that. And I can remember with Sahsha, in a totally different culture, I really had to beat her hands off of the railing and kick her out of the house to get her to go to work.

She: Wasn't she self-supporting, when you met her?

He: Yeah, but as soon as she thought she had a provider, the last thing in the world she intended to do was work.

She: Did you lead her to believe that you would provide . . .

He: I never led her to believe anything of that nature. And later on she thanked me. There's something missing, that's all I'm saying. The explanation is incomplete.

She: What explanation? No one ever said it was all men's doing. In the car today, I was telling you some of the messages that females received after the war which took them back into the home, back into babies, back into marriage. . . .

He: Where did these messages come from?

She: They came from their sisters and from the men; they came from the whole culture, the economy, from employers, from husbands who wanted everything to go back to normal. To have babies, to have the woman at home taking care of babies. They wanted to feel that they were supporting them. . . .

He: I'll be frank. I've never met a man yet—except a couple of creeps—that thought supporting a wife and family was the greatest thing he could do.

She: There're lots and lots of men . . . who regard that as a rite of passage in their lives.

He: I've just never met any of them.

She: I can't say that I've met any either, but in the literature . . .

He: . . . miserable creatures . . .

She: No, no, they're not miserable creatures. I know from what women have said that their men have said . . .

He: Have they heard correctly?

She: Sure, they've heard correctly. They've been told, "Now I have a job. Now I can support you. Now I want you to stay home. Now we'll have children. My wife mustn't work." And so on. They said it particularly in the '50s, when a sign of a man's success was the ability to support those kinds of notions. Other cultures, the Mexicans, don't want their women to work or be out of the house. The home is where they should be. This is not middle-class.

He: Well, the lumpen intelligentsia that I knew best, I guess they were so poor, none that I knew longed for the female to be . . .

She: B. did not want Terri to work.

He: He was a high school teacher!

She: He was a PhD candidate. She kept having babies. . . .

He: That indicates that he was not willing to accept the discipline required to get a PhD, and he gave up his PhD in order to . . .

She: Balderdash!

He: . . . fulfill his macho mission in life.

She: He gave up his PhD because he developed a passion for teaching science to high school seniors. You can understand that, can't you?

He: He must have been going for a PhD in education.

She: He had dreams of glory, a PhD in philosophy, and he could have done it, but he *and* Terri kept having babies. So there's one. C.'s another one.

He: C.! The biggest phony that ever drew breath. He didn't want you to work, but if you'd walked the streets and not had to say where you'd gotten the money, he'd have been delighted.

She: No, he wouldn't. Why do you say that?

He: He didn't want to be poor.

She: But he wanted to know exactly where I was from eight in the morning until four, to know that I was safely there doing any kind of Mickey Mouse stuff. It was okay temporarily for me to work for *our* future. But I couldn't be in something that fascinated me, interested me, kept me past four o'clock. I couldn't be in anything kooky or flamboyant or exciting. That would make him jealous. And it seems to me, you always think of C. as some sort of bizarre evil from which I have fled, but he fits right into the period, perfectly.

He: Well, you knew him better than I did.

She: I wish you would stop comparing me to R. because her attitude shocked me.

He: It did?

She: I thought she was lazy, purposeless, selfish, amoral, decadent. . . .

He: You didn't behave much differently.

She: That's not true. I had been working for many years . . . at the point where she was saying that she didn't want to go to work teaching, I had racked up about seven years of working because the man said he needed it, and it was for our future. And while I fought that and felt bitter about it, I did it because in a way it did make sense. It seemed fair. You can't have everyone getting the training they need in a household at the same time. But she wasn't willing, ever. . . .

He: Thank God! Think of where I'd be, with my feelings of oughtness, if she had helped. . . .

She: Well, you're lucky she refused.

He: The luckiest thing that ever happened to me.

She: But that isn't what shocked me . . . that she wouldn't do it for you. What shocked me was that she wouldn't support herself. And I don't think you're being fair to me. My difficulty with C. was that he wouldn't support *himself*—he made me do it. Only rarely did he work until he received his PhD. I was raised up to believe that everyone should support himself.

He: Your mother must have given you a pretty powerful image of someone who wouldn't do squat.

She: That's not true either! She worked very hard!

He: What did she do? Taking care of two kids is hardly a full day's labor. . . .

She: Three kids. You refuse to accept the middle-class notion that the male goes out and works—not just middle-class—and the woman stays home and takes care of the house and children.

He: But you said that you grew up believing that everyone should support him- or herself. . . .

She: I grew up with a double message.

He: I'll say you did!

She: My mother told me of all the marvelous deeds of the grandmothers. My father told me of how his mother was a businesswoman who supported the family. They obviously approved of this. My father's sister was a high school principal. They came from a long line of vigorous, hardworking, money-producing females. My father didn't want my mother to work. He wanted her to stay home and do what she wanted to do. She *seemed* to want to take care of the children and grow plants. Although something made her bitter and angry. She thought she wanted to be a mother and decorate the house. And perhaps something in the childhood of working mothers made them choose another way.

He: And not even engage in good works?

She: My mother was pathologically shy. And you have to honor that too. She said to me, "Not this. Don't do as I do. Get yourself prepared to work." And she said it many, many times.

He: But you didn't.

She: No, I didn't. But you see, I graduated from high school into the war, and I worked right away, in a menial job, which enabled me to go to college, so that I didn't have to take my father's money. That was the first step. I was not going to take a man's pay and be beholden to him.

He: But when you went to college, it wasn't to prepare yourself to work.

She: I didn't want to prepare myself to work. This is the mysterious miasma of the war years and the '50s, which I can't explain. There was no work I wanted to do. I *never*, at that time, wanted to prepare myself for work. Not until I had to. I learned how to take shorthand and how to type, business methods, but I didn't want to work. I wanted to earn just enough to enable me to go to college. Forever.

He: So you didn't want to be independent?

She: I *was* independent.

He: You did not project yourself into the future.

She: I didn't want to be successful.

He: You were independent as long as you were young, had good health.

She: Yes, that's all I wanted.

He: But you never thought about getting old. . . .

She: O, heavens, no! I also didn't want children.

He: When did you develop a passion for children?

She: It's the old perversity—I didn't want children until I found out in my first marriage that it was perhaps impossible.

He: You remind me of that James Dean movie *Rebel without a Cause*. You had no cause, no ideology; you had nothing in mind. . . .

She: Did you?

He: I wasn't a rebel. The only thing I had was my hatred of the middle class.

She: That's a purpose in life?

He: I loathed them.

She: I wasn't a rebel. I was trying very hard, with my first marriage, to do what was expected of me. To marry someone virtuous, good, and to begin producing babies, train them up to be good citizens, appoint a house, and so forth. And thank goodness, I didn't get pregnant.

He: You had read a lot about famous women and men. I always dreamed of being great. Even as a poor boy, with no . . .

She: Great like whom?

He: Napoleon! Alexander the Great. I dreamed even as a child of heroic acts.

She: How did you hear about them, the heroes?

He: Simple little things I would read . . .

She: Earlier, before the war, I wanted to be Joan of Arc, and Jo March, and a champion diver.

He: But how could you do that getting pregnant, appointing a house, and raising up children to be good citizens?

She: They're not necessarily mutually exclusive.

He: Seems to me they are. How do you square that circle?

She: You don't *have* to have a garret, be tortured on the rack. . . .

He: No, but you have to work hard, be ruthless. . . .

She: That's a very male idea of . . .

He: I don't know of any female who's done something who . . .

She: There are female writers who simply have a room, and time.

He: But you didn't consider yourself a writer, did you?

She: I was totally mindless, purposeless, and lost. Is that what you want me to say? It's true.

He: It might be true, but that isn't what I want you to say. I don't care what you say.

She: I wanted to be able to play Bach's Two-Part Inventions without the music, read all of Freud, lie in the sun, be less tense with people who had brains—really very simple aims. I no longer wanted to be Joan of Arc with a modern mission, or a champion diver. That was all over by the time the war was ended.

He: You'd given up your dreams of glory.

She: Temporarily.

He: What was the compensation? What did you get in return?

She: I didn't think of it in those terms. I felt lost and unhappy. I thought that if someone loved me and wanted to be with me, that was kind of nice. The trouble was, I didn't want to be with him after a while. I keep trying to explain to you that the war was damaging for a lot of people. . . .

He: But why you?

She: Probably because my uncle was killed at the beginning. And other kids I knew. I had trouble accepting that finality of death. And during that confused period of postwar, all I wanted to do was read and study, to get along, and I felt relieved that during the late '40s, someone who loved me was willing to support me.

He: How curious!

She: What's curious about it?

He: With my background, it seems curious, although I'm sure there were millions like you.

She: Your mother probably felt contempt and fury at your

father because he couldn't support her. I've run into this again and again in the Mexican American culture—the fury these hardworking women feel toward a male who produces nothing for the household. They were expensive appendages. They took food from the children. I don't know enough about feminism and its history to say why my great-grandmother was capable of leaving her husband, who beat her, and traveling all the way across the U.S., when I was even frightened to drive a Ford as far as Reno on the first leg of my first journey to the East Coast. I don't know what conveyance she used, but she brought three children, had no money, had no hope of a job. . . .

He: No Social Security . . .

She: No one to support her at the other end, confident (afraid but confident) that she was doing what was right. I don't know what happened between that time and my time except that women acquired the vote.

He: I suppose you realize that a lot of my questioning comes from a remembered hostility toward the middle class.

She: She was middle-class. Would you have been hostile to her?

He: No, probably not. Not the hardworking middle class. Except for my father, I never knew anyone who didn't work. That's what one did.

She: Well, just because they did it doesn't mean that it's necessary or right or proper for all people at all times.

He: My dear, I couldn't agree more. I'm probing because I find it interesting—if you came from a wealthy family, I wouldn't have any questions at all.

She: Because of a tradition of not working . . .

He: You could rationally expect to be cared for, and money was no object . . . I never asked Lucy Sutherland why she didn't work. She inherited a lot of money. It was never an issue with her.

She: Well, believe me, it was never an issue with any of the women of that time, no matter what background. During the time I was in graduate school . . . I never heard any women talk about how they were going to support themselves. It was enough just to work as a waitress and pay your room and board. What difference did the future make? It made no difference at all. They were doing then what they wanted to do, and although it didn't make them happy, they continued to do it because what was offered out there in trade or business or teaching seemed too awful.

He: Maybe that's it. You're beginning to get down to it. Maybe all of you were making a rational response to the job market.

She: I thought I was.

He: You could bust your ass and never get anywhere.

She: If I had received my teaching credential, which was at that time improbable, because I had sensors out to the Education Department, which they could detect from afar.

He: But you had no vision of the ability to go onward and upward . . . you looked out and didn't see a career you wanted.

She: Onward and upward where?

He: That's the point. The reason you didn't have any conception of onward and upward was that no one came and tried to recruit you, or said, "Hey if you'll join our firm, we'll put you on the fast track because you're bright."

She: Come, now, had anyone said "firm" I would have turned away. . . .

He: *You* might have, but we're talking about a whole generation.

She: . . . a generation for whom the initials NAM were polluted.

He: If a union organizer had come to you and said you could rise in the AFL-CIO—there was no career which you found desirable?

She: None. I didn't want to rise, or be out there with other people, or compete. No. Too visible.

He: All right—you explain to me why no practical response other than having someone take care of you was of any interest to you.

She: I didn't have a practical response to being taken care of. I was asked by a professor if I would like to spend the summer in Europe. Had I been interested in being taken care of, the practical response would have been to say yes.

I was too scared. If I'd had a sense of adventure, of risk, it would have been a good idea to go. He would have taken care of me.

He: What's rather interesting, then, is that when anything having to do with the future came up, you just blanked it out.

She: I never thought about the future.

He: Almost every woman does.

She: Did you?

He: Of course! I thought about it constantly. Everyone I knew [in college] thought about it.

She: Women?

He: No, but the men thought about it constantly.

She: Because they were going to be asked to support the women.

He: Don't you think it rather interesting that no career seemed desirable to you?

She: Yes, it's peculiar. I certainly didn't want to be a surgeon or a doctor, or develop Vitamin E, or be a teacher. There was nothing. I wanted to study ideas but not resolve anything. I think I knew I couldn't. I wanted to do what I was doing, which was study.

He: But obviously you couldn't do that forever.

She: There were people [I knew in college] who did it forever. While we were studying and working part-time, we were waiting for some really interesting man to come along.

Less and less likely as the years went by. This man would descend with a means of livelihood and provide new interest.

He: That was the agenda.

She: And in that tiny world, it had to be someone you'd want to risk your genes with. I never knew anyone at that time (female, that is) who wanted to *become* anything. I think, for the man, it was a rum deal.

He: That might have been, but it turned out to have been a rummer deal for the woman. They're the ones who got screwed in the end.

She: So to speak. But I think that you should realize that, at least for me, it was an unconscious time.

He: But just because it was unconscious, at some level you made decisions, and I think it's interesting trying to figure out at what level those decisions were made. Every human being makes decisions constantly about the future.

She: I think you're wrong. I deliberately did not participate in the training program to become an executive in the [trust company], which I could have done because I did those things well and fast. I said no. I like the level (lowest) where I am. Go away. I didn't become a serious major in anything. Graduate work, I just fell into. Graduate work which even passionate graduate students assured me would lead nowhere. One of the enticements to marriage with M. was that he would allow me to continue what I was doing and be pleased that I did so.

He: One of the curious things about this conversation is that I would assume that you would be passionately interested in your own autobiography and yet in this area, you are very resistant to examining it.

She: I'm not resistant to examining that blank period, but since it was blank then, it's even more blank now. It was blank for a long time.

He: So you say it was blank, and that's it!

She: I hear that it was blank for a lot of women.

He: That might be, but you and I know it wasn't blank. Lots of things were going on, and what seems curious is that you are incurious about finding out about them.

She: I'm not incurious. I'm saying that you can't be very curious about a blank. And actually, I mine that period a lot because . . .

He: How do you mine it if it's a blank?

She: What I seemed to be doing was not what I was doing. In your terms, I was doing nothing, but again and again I realize that I was paying close attention to a state of double consciousness, the state of existing, the nausea of the existentialists. I knew no women who were on their way to something. I did know a few who were concentrating on feeling their existence, mentally. Hard to explain. Did you know any of the first kind?

He: Let me think. Yeah, Rena B. She was on her way to becoming a PhD, and she became a full professor someplace.

She: I never heard of her.

He: That woman historian, that tall, beautiful one.

She: Susie. She was married, had a child. Her husband made good money and did not inquire into her affairs.

He: I knew another one, ended up teaching at Cal State. Died of cancer. Who were the sentient, aware keepers of the faith during the '50s?

She: In the '50s I was supporting a husband, back East and in Europe. No one kept the faith.

He: In that whole decade they were silent?

She: Not until the publication, I think in the '60s, of *The Feminine Mystique*—there was nothing.

He: In England, France?

She: I don't recall.

He: Italy? South America?

She: I don't know, but I did not read anything illuminating. With the publication of that book, not all at once but little by little, women began reading and said, "Aha, that's what's been happening to me."

He: So *The Feminine Mystique* was really an important book.

She: Very important. And I didn't read it until last year.

He: It was written in '56, and you didn't read it for twenty-four years? That's weird! Maybe you didn't have to read it because you were participating in that culture.

She: I was reading other things. I was reading *The Second Sex*, which was very important to me in the '50s and was

then and later a tonier book, more literary. It's a more difficult feminine-mystique book, deeper. It has less to do with
America and more to do with all women. I belonged to a set
of people who weren't reading *The Feminine Mystique* for
snob reasons.

He: I read *The Second Sex* the year it was published.

She: I probably did too. I read it three or four times. I
needed it.

He: I consider myself an early feminist. Far earlier than
you. In fact, I was a feminist throughout the '50s.

She: I wasn't ready to take that stance in the New York
academic environment. You just wanted them to get off
your back.

He: But I believe that no female should be a deadbeat,
supported human being.

She: But of the females you knew, which ones could you
have encouraged to become something more than they were?

He: I encouraged all of them.

She: We knew so many females who seemed to be stuck.

He: I was shocked at Meg.

She: Hopeless. Marvelous intelligence.

He: She was giving up everything she had worked for to
run off with a man. And I told her so. I thought she should
finish her degree at Columbia. She wasn't interested. I suppose I met the first women who weren't the kind you're talking about in the union movement.

She: You were excited, thrilled and fell in love with them?

He: No, but I certainly admired them.

She: Yes, you should. But they weren't the first. There was Susan.

He: And there were some in politics that I thought were pretty good. The difference between women in politics and the women in the union movement is that women in politics always worked for a male. The women involved in political action, community-organizing unions were the first women I'd met who worked for themselves.

She: I knew a number of women in the union movement in my teaching days, and I don't know whether I admire them. They loved doing it more than they loved teaching. Unionizing, rushing off to conventions.

He: ... Can you name me any movement—including the American Revolution—where someone wouldn't be able to say that—the crops are rotting in the fields, the wife and children are being ignored, while you're out there rabble-rousing. There's no food on the table—you got yourself fired from your job down at the mine or the mill.

She: What has been gained?

He: In all of this?

She: For me, very little.

He: That may be true for you, but looking back over the history of organization, I am a passionate believer in organizing in all industry—on the docks, in the mines, factories, offices, and in the schools.

She: No one knows teachers better than I do, and many

should be fired, and they shouldn't be protected by a union. They are goof-offs, and they are stupid. They're mean to the kids, and they don't learn anything.

He: You're talking about American industry, American society.

She: But the union, which organizes to better the conditions of teachers, is the organization which would protect these teachers.

He: That's the same argument you give against abolishing slavery. The point is, organized people are more capable of change than disorganized, weak people. Lord Acton said, etc., "Lack of power corrupts, and absolute lack of power corrupts absolutely."

She: I have heard so many teachers say, "They can't do that to me because I'm a member of a union," and I think, "By God, they ought to do that to you. No matter what you're a member of."

He: That's right. But what you don't seem to realize is that the union is an important organization to change teacher behavior—in fact more important than the bloody school district.

She: No union ever protected me against a school district.

He: Well, you're a pain in the ass. Why would any union leader, knowing you and your history, do anything to help you?

She: What's more important?

He: Teaching conditions, the number of kids in the classroom. Tons of things are more important. That's like the people who would come in and want a resolution to recognize Red China, and I would rule all those motions out of order. They would call me a fascist.

She: I thought all that political ideology was irrelevant for the union.

He: One can't organize without an organizer.

She: I know—I read the union news. The guys play politics, and the ladies have a ball.

He: I see—well, when you go back and listen to this tape, it will probably tell you a lot about the conditions of women. Your attitude toward organization and your focusing on the now without looking at a larger social organization in which to judge one's activities, and the value you place on these things probably has a relationship to the blankness of the '50s.

She: I don't think you're being fair. The four-year-old is now.

He: I've heard Chicano educators say, "What are you going to do about this generation of kids?" Very responsible people were writing this generation off.

She: The teacher in the classroom is not writing this generation off.

He: There was no one out there to help the eight- and nine-year-olds. They said, "You can't save them; they're gone."

She: You mean bilingual education.

He: Whatever it was—getting teachers ready for the first and second graders so that they didn't lose them. Taking whatever slender resources they had and putting it where they thought they'd get the biggest payoff. It's making the difficult choices. There ain't no such thing as free lunch in this world, socially, individually, or any other way. And you might write off a school district. You might write off fifty classrooms out of a hundred. That's what revolutionaries, organizers, do all the time. The women too. The Pankhursts of this world. The principle of organization is the same whether it's women or men, whether you're organizing teachers or a protest about El Salvador.

She: We are looking at it from different points of view. The women I knew who were union organizers, in spite of the district, were so excited by the glamour of this new challenge . . .

He: So!

She: I'm trying to question whether what you say is right. . . .

He: I don't know whether it's right. . . .

She: I don't want to talk more about it. It's getting me mad. You have always said that large movements are more important than small classrooms and what goes on there. I don't believe that. I've never believed it. Although my father told me the same thing. And he was a complicated failure. He's dead, and he lived a long time. He believed that massive organization benefits mankind. And he was right, but he didn't pay attention to small.

He: I think if you'll go back and review what we've said, I have at no time said that union organization is more important than being a good classroom teacher. Both are important.

She: No one person did both.

He: That's right. People do different things.

She: But you started this tape by saying, "Why don't women do more?"

He: I think that's a good question. Would you like to be back in the '50s? Do you think that was a great period for females?

She: It wasn't a great period for anybody. There was a reaction, a disappointment, a sorrow—homes were established, families raised, the women worked hard, and so did the men, and then the pendulum moved—and the women asked, "What am I doing? It's not enough." Not enough for the individual. After the war it would have been really eccentric to have the man you loved home safe and to say to him, "Sorry, buster, but I'm going to go out and organize." There was a great sigh of relief, and after relief you find perhaps you've made a mistake to concentrate and confine your activities.

He: Can you give me any history of previous wars or what women did in other societies after a war? If what you say is right, maybe it was natural—but perhaps it was bizarre, totally atypical. I don't know. It seems to me that's something you should be looking at for answers.

She: You look at large, and I look at . . .

He: Micro and macro. Both are very valuable. Neither is more valuable than the other, and both are necessary. It's like theoretical and experimental physics. One can't exist without the other.

She: I'm not sure you believe that. If you did, you would not say of a woman who was wife, mother, and teacher, and had been for many years, "What *else* is she doing? Why doesn't she do more?" It took me a while to learn that I couldn't do the macro and still attend to the micro. In the '60s, I got the message that I was an inferior person, no matter what I did, if I merely concentrated on my children at home and the thirty children in the classroom.

He: I knew lots of women who did that—dealt with their families, dealt with their classrooms, and passionately sustained the union: "Here's my money—you go out there and fight on those barricades. If there's ever a strike vote, you don't have to worry about me."

She: Not me. I had a psychic disability for large fights. They made me sick.

He: Well, that's just who you are.

She: That's who I became after one long, desperate, large fight over custody. I don't want to march for anything . . .

the confrontation with mass opposition sickens me. The last fight I can think of that might have been worth it was the vote, and I was born just postvictory.

He: Fine. That's just your view of it. I don't think there are many women who would agree with you. Very few who consider themselves feminists.

She: At present, the only fight I can think of which might involve my mind, and certainly my body, is the right to an abortion.

He: I can't think of any activist female who would agree with you. They'd all disagree, every one of them.

She: I'm not an activist female, and the curious thing is that insofar as my father knew what he was doing, he hoped he was creating an activist female. He gave me the literature, explained the holy glory of union activities, took me to view prisons, and introduced me to prisoners. He preached brotherhood and risking all for one's right-thinking comrades.

He: Well, I think that you would probably look at me and think that everything I [believe] is something you would disagree with. . . .

She: I don't like this tape.

He: It's a good tape.

She: It's not fair.

He: What do you mean, it's not fair?

She: You're getting irritated. . . .

He: I'm not getting irritated.

She: You're saying to me that it's not enough to have done

what I did, in the period of time I did it. I should have done more. And people have always said I should have done more. I should have been a better wife, a better mother, etc.

He: If I say that I think you should have supported the union movement, it's because I believe that that was what you should have done in support of your fellow teachers.

She: I paid my dues, I voted correctly, I went out on strike, but each time I entered a fight, my classroom suffered. I got sick, and there were others who did it better.

In car

She: In this book we're writing, so far there's too much talk about sex.

He: I thought that was what it was all about.

She: That's not what I had in mind. We were talking about male-female friendships.

He: What other kind of friendship is there?

She: See, there you go.

He: I'm playing protagonist. If we had no sexual difficulties, we probably would have very few other difficulties. You think I interrupt you occasionally, and I'm too quick to tell you how smart I am; I do not allow you to get into a low dudgeon and put me down whenever I suggest something—wry face, arms akimbo—the many techniques you have of controlling my behavior. You flounce occasionally.

She: You don't want me to do that anymore? Won't you miss it?

He: I just see you doing it, and I stop it. . . . For instance, you were well on your way to wrecking this trip today by saying, "Well, is the only reason we're going to Gaviota is to get back?"

She: But that cuts right down the center between masculine and feminine.

He: It's linear versus Gestalt.

She: But you had made the statement "We'd better get going so we can get back." Now, could anything be more stupid?

He: We agreed that we would leave when you got home from work. And I had buttoned up [my work], had showered, shaved, tied, and shoed. I was ready to go. And I didn't want to make a trip to the North Pole out of it.

She: But how can you enjoy someplace when you go there with the idea of getting back from it?

He: I find that when I have x number of hours for an activity, then I can throw myself into that activity totally!

She: This is our tempo problem.

He: I need the security of a beginning and an end so that I can devote myself to other things in between. If I plan, then I can assume it won't be midnight when we get back.

She: That would be terrible, wouldn't it?

He: The primary scarcity that we have is time. In our lives, our days, and all the days of our years. If we didn't live in time, we wouldn't have to apportion it. And remember that every moment you spend in one thing has an opportunity cost when you could be doing something else.

She: It sounds frantic, the way you put it.

He: It's not frantic. It's philosophical. It's the way the external world is structured, and there's nothing one can do about it. So one accepts that, and one is able to live one's life in harmony with philosophical principles.

She: I have nothing to say. And you have finished.

He: That is a decision you made, not I.

She: You have stated your philosophical position, and I don't have anything to add except a sense that you have more time if you don't worry about time at all. However, you may get very little done. But there is little that I want to get done.

He: I see. For the rest of your life?

She: For the rest of my life.

He: I have a ton of things I want to do.

She: But if you had four times the time, you'd still be in a hurry.

He: I haven't been rushing about today. I've been relaxed. Maybe that time sense will cause us real trouble. The fact that I have a lot of things I want to do and you have few if any you want to do.

She: There are books I want to read, but rushing won't get them read. There's plenty of time. . . . My ambition is minor. Sorry.

He: That's your business, not mine. I'm willing to accept the fact that you don't want to do much. You should be able to accept the fact that I'm wanting to do a hell of a lot.

She: We're talking about our time together. When we're

apart, it doesn't matter if you budget your time to the second and I don't budget even a minute of my day.

He: I find you most animated, most interested and interesting, when you're most deeply involved in your work. And I think that you will find that without work, and serious work, that all the time that you have is not going to be nearly as satisfying to you as you might imagine. I think humans need work. . . . Productivity is the hallmark of practically every literary giant in history. Flaubert is the rare exception. You can go right down the line—the important writers are productive. Writers with small output have small reputations.

She: I don't like this conversation.

TELEPHONE

He: I agree, marriage is a bummer for women because men are always making demands on her and they do complain a lot and more and more, but they have to be supported. . . . They have to screw for their living. . . .

She: Also there's fatherhood. The fathers want to be close to their children, and they still have a lot of regard for their females. They love them. So it's usually regarded as a difficult time, and out the other side of it, they're startled to find that they have changed. The difficulties may go on for years and years. The women have most concern over all of the growing problems, all the schoolwork, fears, and troubles of their children. They continue to be much more involved than the men. The bed becomes trite or dull. The man complains about it. I bought Nancy Friday's *Men in Love*, and I noticed there's much comment about how in the beginning it was wonderful. When the children come, the wife just doesn't want to anymore, and fantasies appear. Their fantasies are much appointed and plumped up by *Playboy* and *Penthouse*.

He: That leads me to some other questions. These might not seem friendly.

She: We are making friendliness a condition of our conversations, are we?

He: No, no. You have a scholarly interest in the physical and emotional functionings of males, but it's not something that's really of first-level interest to you. You like to treat males more as abstractions which you endow with various characteristics and are relatively indifferent to who they actually are.

She: That's probably not true.

He: I think you have a low level of curiosity about my physical reactions, much lower than I have of yours.

She: Seems to me they *are* what they do, what they say, what they eat, how they move, and whether or not they lick the backs of spoons.

He: I think that you're not only a typical woman but a sensitive one, and our typicality, if there is such a word, is most interesting to observe. I think the only way you're not typical is in your level of self-awareness, self-observation, and an amazing candor.

She: You believe I don't see the consequences!

He: Therefore you go blundering onward.

She: I'm curious what happens if you throw into the game an observation which is candid. You get an amazing amount of ripple.

He: Yes. You also, I find, are very uncurious about the way you respond in a sexual sense. You're very interested in humidity, pressure, wind, temperature—all of those things. But you aren't very interested in tastes—food, alcohol. You're not a sensualist. Are you?

She: As D. H. Lawrence said somewhere—"The deepest sensuality is the search for truth." I can remember that the worst one graduate student could say of another in the '50s was "He/she is not a sensualist." It was a ferocious, scathing indictment, and I think it usually meant that he/she was interested in a career and didn't screw much.

He: What's a sensualist?

She: Someone who really delights in the senses. That's a liberal meaning and quite accurate. But we have hearing and seeing as well as taste.

He: You certainly do respond to music more powerfully than I do.

She: We both love music, but I go overboard. And I love warmth, love to be immersed in water, and *sun*! O! Made love to by the sun! Food I can take or leave.

He: Another question. Your need for the unexpected in sex, which you've mentioned on numerous occasions. Yet I've watched you in other things, and you desire the expected when I come home, in the constancy of love, the warmth of physical contact. All those other things that you just wanted repeated in almost exactly the same way. Almost ritualistically.

She: I can't explain it. I don't ask that I be moved to tears *every* time I hear Pachelbel or "The Butcher Boy." It seems to me that certain rituals are deeply comforting, even sensual. I've known men who, as soon as they find out that something works, grind away at it the next night, thus arousing in me an almost motherly concern for the pathos of the act. That's a sure way to kill it. One of the difficulties of the vibrator is that your own hand is operating it when you're doing it to yourself, and it's difficult to feel mystery in your own hand.

He: Why do you need mystery? Do you need fantasy?

She: No, it's a fantasyless unexpectedness.

He: Why unexpectedness in this area of your life and not another?

She: Don't you need it? Do you like to do the same thing over and over again?

He: As long as it's pleasurable.

She: But it is pleasurable to repeat?

He: Well, if it happened twice, or three times, it would be boredom. But with you it's not boredom which sets in; it's your need for not knowing.

She: May I inject a testimonial to you? You are seldom boring. Within the general boundaries of bed, of doing it, you arrive at it in many different ways, and different ways within small known ways. Do you do that deliberately? Or instinctively?

He: Sort of instinctively, but sometimes all the ways are unsuccessful as far as you're concerned. Occasionally I may arouse you, but generally not. So I guess the question is, is arousal the purpose of the activity? New question: Since purposiveness, in any of its guises, is suspect to you, why do it at all?

She: I sometimes wonder. And yes, arousal *is* the purpose. But aiming always for orgasm is a great burden. The goal consumes the pleasure and makes me wonder where all my other senses are and if they're up to something odd or more interesting.

He: You're lying there wondering, "Why am I doing this?"

She: I know why I'm doing it.

He: Because *I* want to.

She: You know how much trouble I've given you about preparing every detail of a trip in advance? Preparing for a destination, knowing where we're going and what we'll take with us and where we'll be when we get there, removes some of the spontaneity of simply adventuring. It's a nice automobile. We could take any road, arrive at any town, anytime, find that we have no place to stay, and see what we do with that. That would be fun. We might have stomachaches, backaches, get caught in a thunderstorm.

He: Those were my questions. Not very satisfactory answers, I must say.

She: I have often wished I weren't that way. The expectations are always clear, the setting is there, and we go from A to B. I wish I could jump into that with fervor and excitement. So do you.

He: Why would I rather make love to you, whether it's unsatisfactory or boring, than with anyone else?

She: That is a question which you must answer. I don't think you should look too closely into it. In Friday's *Men in*

Love, the men want the women more than the women want the men. They want to be the instrument of the women's pleasure. They will bind themselves with marriage, children, and early death and keep trying. I hope you go on feeling that way.

He: So do I. It's a very pleasant way to feel.

She: Good-night, dear.

TELEPHONE

He: The reason you've never had to put yourself out is that men are enthralled, and I must confess that I desire to satisfy you.

She: That is a dear thing to say.

He: But of course you don't like that.

She: Sometimes I like it very much.

He: But most of the time you find it a burden.

She: I had dinner tonight with Sally and her roommates. I wanted to ask them some of the questions which we've been asking each other. I told them I was doing a book and was wondering whether I could be a spokeswoman for feminism just because I've read a lot of books. I moved the furniture around a bit and asked, "Supposing there was a woman with a nursing child and a two-and-a-half-year-old, and her husband wanted sex five times a night." I got a three-way scream: *"Five times a night!"* They said, "Let him masturbate," "Tell him to go get it someplace else," "That's quite abnormal," "Two people should accommodate each other, and that sounds like service at a pump," and "How long and of what quality is each of the five?" And little Samual has his chin on the table, his ears growing out over the soup bowl, eyes darting from woman to woman. They have volunteered to be my sounding board as a check against our rampant theorizing.

He: Good.

Restaurant

He: You were a depressive. You never hid it from me. You just collapsed all over the place. But I didn't mind because of that quality of candor. And I'll tell you this: You were a better screw when you were depressed than any other time because you were so absolutely open, yielding, accepting. You were earth-body.

She: You want me to get depressed again?

He: No, no, no, no, no. There were lots of things that weren't very good about it. On balance, the morning after tended to dissipate the joys of the night. But they were there. And why? Because you were vulnerable.

She: And I'm no good when I'm not vulnerable?

He: When I came staggering in here last week, you were more passionate, loving, tender the farther I sank into the Slough of Despond.

She: I think we'll always be very helpful to each other in our infirmities. Don't you think so?

He: Probably. But I don't think it speaks well for either of our characters. It's the vulture part of our natures.

She: True. I felt no impulse toward looking for a mate. There was always *someone* around, but I never had the feeling that there was *that* person out there who could tolerate me, and vice versa. I no longer believed in that sort of existence. I *wanted* to be alone. There were days when I didn't even want my kids to come home. I didn't want harm to befall them. I wanted them to go stay with some other family.

He: When you fell into depression, and even suicidal, what precipitated that?

She: Sometimes . . . an overabsorption in sex. Sometimes nothing that I could see.

He: They were visitations from on high?

She: I was helped toward a period of almost permanent depression by your sudden refusal to see or talk to me. I was clouded for almost a year.

He: But it happened on more than that occasion.

She: Yes.

He: Why?

She: You told me the other day that you had it all figured out, that it was inherited, genetic, hormonal, and that I should get pills in readiness for the next time.

He: That's probably true.

She: I'm not takin' no pill. I'll run my head off rather than take pills.

He: That doesn't mean that you're not genetically predisposed.

She: I believe that depressions are not *caused* in any understandable sense.

He: They just happen. There's a machine going around in you, and every seventh year and six days . . .

She: It isn't regular or cyclical. The last couple of days, in response to spring, I have been full of health, feeling glorious. The world is a fragrant, colored, smelly place. On another day, perhaps in response to weather, I may feel that there's nothing worth reading, doing, talking about. The dips now are not as low—the euphoria is more intellectual. I don't see any reason to do anything about it.

He: No, not if the lows have shallowed out and the highs are still there.

She: There are many more things that amuse me now. I can be amused by chaos, by self-flagellation, when I look at myself and say, "Hmm, what an idiot! What a moron! What a defective person!" This now amuses me. It didn't once.

He: Tell me, are you able to talk about your new body awareness?

She: I haven't been doing anything that I'd not done before. It's just that I haven't been paying attention for a long time.

He: But you're more aware now?

She: I was always aware that I had a clitoris, but I never had a vibrator before. And it wasn't spring. It's not as much fun in the rain.

He: But the sun is shining, and the birds are singing. . . .

She: Also I have a response to pornography which my sisters would not approve.

He: Is that new?

She: No, it is ur-alt. It's always been there. It's nothing I've been proud of, but it's there, always was, and always will be.

He: Why shouldn't you be proud of it?

She: No pride is justified. Even if I were to become a lesbian and join in their political posture, I don't see how I'd grow out of it.

He: When you say pornography, what kind of pornography? Reading Anaïs Nin? Visual?

She: No, I doubt if I would enjoy watching it. I like to read about it.

He: Whom do you like?

She: O, pick a book. It's everywhere. I am not deprived. *Men in Love* is sometimes pornographic. What was I reading recently? Probably I was reading about all the brutalities—the deformed feet and suttee in *Gyn/Ecology*. I appreciate all the excuses. I have, as you've often said, a morbid curiosity and a morbid bent. I like to read about women being brutally tamed.

He: And *The Story of O* didn't bother you much? Turned you on like crazy.

She: Turn on? *The Story of O* did much to me. It started me thinking about freedom and its relation to slavery, much more so than *The Grand Inquisitor*. It was personal. I can imagine myself being O and giving up my freedom for a life of subjection to male wishes. It was exciting to wonder if she would stop , rebel, would she throw up, would she make a break, and what would they think of next, they who are as enslaved as she. What they think of next is so degrading.

He: That excites you . . . ?

She: Yes, but I could not defend *O* because of its useful-ness in bringing me to reconsider the question of freedom versus slavery. That's nonsense. I could get that elsewhere. And I'm not going to say anything about "woman is . . ." It's an individual matter.

He: The reason I can't say anything about what man is is that I haven't the vaguest idea.

She: Women's fantasies sometimes contain rape, torture, etc., but I don't know whether their parents made them that way, whether they're "naturally" so, whether it is a subcon-scious programming, or none of these. Perhaps we're a group of freaks. I can remember when I lived in a house which I left when I was eight, I used to imagine that I was tied to a stake. I didn't read cowboy stories; there was no TV. This tree was so situated that it was out of the view of any win-dow in the house. I would writhe until I had an orgasm. One of my favorite books was a large children's book which told the story of Joan of Arc.

He: That's strange. Do you know when I discovered orgasm?

She: By pulling on it?

He: No. Climbing ropes in grade school. And I'd ask the

other kids, "Did something funny happen to you when you climbed?" And I'd climb that rope ten times a day.

But thinking back on my days on the kindergarten playground, when I was the only kid going around wondering what in God's name was happening to me, leads me to believe that it is not psychic but genetic. I could have become a murderer, a leader of men, or a PhD. It was a powerful physical drive that has manifested itself in all sorts of ways.

She: O, yes. The horses I rode on Saturday in riding school usually had Western saddles with a hill which fitted into me. A slow walk with the dullest horse was the best. Galloping was not as satisfactory. I used to ask for a wreck of a horse with one blind eye. No one else asked for him. I'd be left behind and savor my pleasure.

He: Yes, after the rope discovery I started having orgasms from all sorts of things. Again and again. Then I discovered masturbation. When I was in my early twenties, I used to gamble in the Chinese gambling houses, and if I either won or lost a large bet, I'd have an orgasm.

She: You didn't limit your pleasure.

He: But peak sexual response to cultural beauty didn't come until I was thirty-five.

She: That's interesting. Orgasm from concertos and opera at sunset occurred for me in Europe in the same years.

He: I think it's that we were abstracted then.

She: Yes, we were able to turn wholeheartedly, whole-bodied, to the experience. We didn't even have the distraction of being in a known environment.

He: And we were older. The body did not react as impetuously or as rapidly. There's been a dramatic diminution in my sexual responses.

She: Has there? When? Where?

BED

SCENE: HE and SHE in bed with tape recorder.

TIME: A night in April, in California in the 1980s

She: Sometime we're going to have to talk on tape about this agreement we've signed.

He: The content of these tapes should appear in a book, and if the content is as outrageous as the contract, it's going to outrage some people . . . one thing I find fascinating, and which makes me fall in love with you every time I think of it, is . . . where did you get the audacity (I wouldn't call it courage) to try something like that? The sheer genius? When I go back over all of our arguments, all the times when we were thrashing about on the issue of your bending your will to another, other figures loomed up, shadows from the past. If we did something together, all the other men you'd done it with interposed themselves.

She: Do you remember when I wrote that letter offering myself as mistress? I wrote it because I was angry at myself for feeling miserable. I sat down and in the petulant heat

wrote a suggestion. I got carried away at the typewriter because it was so much fun . . .

He: . . . as is your wont . . .

She: . . . so much fun to give away all of my freedom and
to give up all my other roles of feminist, analyst of what was
happening to me and other women—to just throw it away
and be paid for all I had previously, supposedly, done out of
love. What's a letter? *Send it.* He'll either never respond,
or he'll laugh. I didn't expect you to accept it.

He: I thought it was the greatest offer I'd ever received.

She: By phone, immediately, you accepted. And I can remember feeling soaringly happy at the whole antic. For
weeks and weeks after that, I tried out what it felt like to be
a mistress, which I certainly had never been. It's not even a
category available . . .

He: . . . to a modern woman.

She: I, modern woman, went dancing around, took walks,
thought, and wrote not a word of it in my journal. I didn't
want it to be literary. I needed it to be real.

He: You've grown into the role beautifully.

She: There was a big payoff besides happiness. Housing,
money. It's not too fair.

He: Why? Just because you happen to have someone who
is madly in love with you and would give you anything he had?

She: But if you were as penniless as I am, this kind of
agreement wouldn't work at all.

He: You wonder what I'm getting out of this?

She: That question does not usually occur to women. They say, "Why don't you do this, or treat me another way?" They find it hard to ask, "What am I getting out of this?" A home, cutlery, kids, and a man's protection they expect, and then demand more.

He: I never have been penniless, but I don't think it's just a function of the fact that in a relative sense I've become affluent. I'm a lot richer than I can make use of. That is, my worth is a lot greater than my ability to spend money. What puzzles me is, is this new pleasure a function of age, or experience, or what? You're the genius. You're the one who thinks up these delicious ideas.

She: It's surely not an idea I got from reading feminist books. It's perverse.

He: The only thing I can think of which is similar is your former joy in ritual rape. You loved to be raped.

She: Ritualistically.

He: And you love this role. Only this isn't ritualistic. This is real. You might think you can get out of it, but habit will trap you. We'll develop behavior patterns, and you won't be able to escape.

She: I can't right now imagine wanting to escape because nobody wants to go over all of women's battles every day one meets with a man.

He: You were doing that.

She: I'm sure many women do. They work hard and worry hard, but much of their lives is drudgery, and they put their hearts and souls into combat with males. They work on bringing their analysis of the situation up-to-date. I don't want to do that anymore. This is a scheme which allows me . . .

He: . . . freedom.

She: I can still analyze but don't have to do it in my own household.

He: Yes, you can go to meetings, sit with the sisters, and express rage.

She: I've become a mistress.

He: This goes back to a period where women, by being compliant with male wishes, received substantial rewards. They had a position, security. It was an even exchange.

She: This is still true, but the women now wish to eliminate from the exchange all assumption that their bodies are part of the trade. I understand this. They are bargaining from a weak position and would rather not.

He: Modern marriage, or modern living together, doesn't really offer much in the way of an exchange. What does a female get out of being sexually equal to a male? That's not what a sexual union is about. It just doesn't work.

She: Women may spend all their time making decisions and none, or not much, enjoying. Still, the assumption is that this period will pass and men and women will, sometime in the future, have a more easeful lovemaking.

He: It hasn't with us. I have been with you for eighteen years and have never entered your bed reluctantly.

She: Never?

He: Sometimes, when you are enraged, I have wanted to kill you or throw you over the balcony or lock you in the closet. But no matter how enraged you've been, you've always had the wit to compose your differences, and we've never failed to end up snuggled in one another's arms.

She: Breathing smog.

He: Smog brought on by the issue of decision-making. Who has the authority? You were saying, "I've been pushed around by men all my life—father, husband, judges, lovers—and I'm not going to be pushed around anymore."

She: It's insane to have had difficulties for years over the issue of being pushed around and to decide that the way to solve it is to be completely dominated.

He: You could become a lesbian. Women wouldn't push a penis into you.

She: The alternative to being with men is not to turn to women.

He: Being alone is always available. Having companionship, friends, sex, underneath all the love, has a basic element of violence. It is a taking.

She: I'm aware of the violence. It's caused my fear right now of the outside world, where at this moment, in my town, we are asked not to take a nature walk until the killer of last weekend is apprehended. Today is three days after Reagan was shot by yet another nut. We must be the most nonpolitical country in the world. Our presidents are blown away by kooks, people who are acting out TV or movie fiction.

He: What has the general violence to do with the fact that there's a core of violence to sex?

She: Women have made themselves aware of violence and want to decrease it. Yet when they begin to negotiate and raise demands in bed, one possible result is that you, the man, may not want to make love to them anymore.

He: With our agreement, you can just quit, be free. In marriage, there are children, and the social obligations arrive. The biological obligations come and stay. What chance does a couple have to derive maximum pleasure from bed?

She: Did the mistresses of the eighteenth century have children?

He: Sometimes, but usually not. They didn't want them.

She: Didn't want them? Or didn't want illegitimate ones?

He: A pregnant woman is nine months out of action, more or less. A man wants a mistress for pleasure.

She: Yeah, yeah. Did they have status?

He: Of course. If they were smart, they saw to it that they were cared for financially in case the ardor waned.

She: Was it contractual?

He: Yes; there'd be a settlement of some kind.

She: What class was this? How many people?

He: Only a tiny portion. Only the males who could afford

it. No woman in her right mind was going to be a mistress to some impecunious, slack-jawed, ardent male.

She: So what was left to the rest of them was a marriage in poverty, or spinsterhood, or disgrace.

He: Many chose spinsterhood.

She: Because of the perils of pregnancy?

He: And because no proper male presented himself.

She: I'm getting sleepy. It seems strange to be *talking* to you in bed. We haven't done much of that.

He: We have to talk; the tape recorder is on.

She: I'm turning it off.

BED

He: As I was saying, one of the things we need to explore in this book is what I perceive to be the dividends of growing old. I don't like to think of it as growing old . . . the dividends that come from both of us having been through most of life's experiences, children for you, a child for me. For both of us, child-raising. Unsatisfactory marriages. Bad love affairs. Struggles. We are at the point where we're willing to take a few chances, where we can go on an adventure, and when we put it in this book, the readers will be amazed.

She: I seem to remember trying to convince you that it would be an interesting adventure for you to try fidelity. That didn't work out too well.

He: That didn't work out at all.

She: It emasculated you, irritated you, reduced you to less than you thought you ought to be. It was no good at all, and even I backed off from that.

He: That's true. It struck at the roots.

She: There are many who agree that fidelity demanded of, asked of one's mate produces little pits of rot and much jealousy and possessiveness. On the other hand, it's difficult to live with someone, on that basis, to whom one is married. But we are not married, nor are we together constantly. As I pointed out, you have been with me only twenty-six days out of ninety this year.

He: In the summer of '79, I was with you ninety days out of ninety, but we weren't in love the way we are now.

She: Was that the summer we were on the Dong diet?

He: That was the summer your son was causing trouble. He was doing old automobiles. . . . Compared to the way you are now, you weren't much fun to be around. Now you're delightful.

She: I kept saying to you then, and I'll still say, that I was not the one who was experiencing your fidelity. My roots were not being bruised. You were the one who was enduring whatever happens when you, a male, become faithful to a female. I received the reaction, the evidence of your distress. But let's not talk about the summer of '79. It was terrible. We were starving to death in the interest of health. We had a protein deficiency; we were probably producing hypoglycemia. I could look into my head as into a vast canyon of emptiness. That was the summer when I remarked that we were the most boring couple in existence.

BED

She: When [women] begin to negotiate and raise demands in bed, one possible result is that you, the man, may not want to make love to them anymore

He: That's true.

She: You might even be unable to get a hard-on for the first time in eighteen years. The attack may produce a result, and is doing just that, among other lovers.

He: That's true. If you press me too hard, I won't perform. Then I leave.

She: That's a negative power. I can produce a withering of the penis by my demand for something which, possibly, is very unnatural.

He: To me.

She: To you. It doesn't seem to be natural to other men either. I don't think they've begun to answer back yet. There are a few men's liberation groups, but I don't think they've found their literary voice yet.

He: What's going to happen is that you're going to be their voice.

She: I'm not comfortable with that. This book is going to be one couple's voice . . . two people out of many.

He: Perhaps there is no satisfactory sexual relationship

other than arranging the social and economic structure so that both parties receive benefit, a fair and equal exchange.

She: Women have objected for a long time to being the one who services. What is she going to do with this view?

He: What you and I have done is return to an almost eighteenth-century solution.

She: In the eighteenth century, the wife was provided for, raised the children, and kept the house. The mistress was also provided for and gave her body.

He: But after the children were raised, the man did not stay with his wife. He went to stay with his mistress. Generally.

She: I didn't know that.

He: Why would he stay with the wife? She had grandchildren, etc.

She: And was glad to get rid of him. Progeny was what it was all about to begin with.

He: What we've done, because financially we're able to do it, is not available to most couples, either psychologically or financially. How would a young couple of equal financial capability deal with the difficulties of bed? I don't see any solution unless they make a dark and evil pact such as we have. It isn't available within the legal structure of marriage.

She: I believe that legally, in marriage, the man must support and the woman must put out. I'll bet it's in the California Code.

He: It's in no code that I know of.

(Dog jumps onto bed)

She: Hey, I didn't invite you onto the bed! Look at her, sniffing you.

He: One of the reasons she accepts me so completely is that she comes up to me and smells you.

Working out the financial arrangements of satisfactory male-female relationships is not easy. I also feel people meet, grow, express themselves, and then meet again, be free to change . . .

She: Marriage is too constant.

He: There's no end to it. And quite apart from its becoming oppressive by *design*, it happens unconsciously. Each oppresses the other. It's no part of their intention. It just happens.

She: An infinite series of accommodations.

He: One of the reasons you can go into this seemingly demeaning arrangement is that you know you can always just quit, be free. And right now, maybe you could. But in a year, you won't be able to. You'll be trapped, and let's hope you'll be trapped in something that continues to give you pleasure.

She: And you?

He: The same. In marriage, one is trapped, and this doesn't give pleasure. There are children, and the social obligations come. The biological obligations come and stay. . . .

She: We have made a mistress-master contract, and you

stated, I think it was yesterday, that this contract was different from marriage. Today I've been at the library trying to verify that assertion. I tried to find actual marriage codes, but the law library was closed. What I was able to get aplenty, in various books, are the various state grounds for divorce. If something is grounds for divorce, there must be something in the law of marriage which has been violated. Except in states with no-fault divorce. If she refuses, it is grounds for divorce. Also the husband's failure to provide for his legal wife is grounds.

He: Provide what?

She: Everything but spare cash. He must provide doctors, food, dwelling, enough money to run the household. If he doesn't, the wife can sue for divorce, or if she doesn't want a divorce, she can sue for provision of all that stuff which goes with marriage. If that is so, and is still true in the United States, in most states . . .

He: Doesn't the wife have any rights to her husband's hard penis?

She: I believe it's mutual. Usually the complaint is the other way round. And I believe in all states, noncongress is grounds for divorce.

He: C. certainly had plenty of grounds for divorce from you.

She: Yes. I hadn't the faintest idea, when I married, what kind of contract I had made, what was legal and what illegal. I didn't even have a notion that *anything* was legal or illegal.

I knew only that the man was required, under certain conditions, to pay support and alimony. It had not ever occurred to me that the wife *had* to submit, that the man had sexual rights and vice versa. Sounds funny, doesn't it? That a woman has sexual rights? But you can't force a husband to perform. If he can't, he can't, and he can always plead lack of ability. But you *can* force a woman. So what is different about the mistress-master contract?

He: It doesn't involve the state.

She: But that's not the difference we've been feeling.

He: It's an overt stipulated agreement.

She: It's not similar to what one *thinks* one has agreed to in a marriage. . . .

He: But is similar in fact.

She: And perhaps that's because there is a greater wisdom in ancient law and society than there is in the hearts of lovers. Since these rights have seemed to be the best way to work it out, they have been made legal. So what are we doing? What do we think we're doing? Why is it so exciting?

He: Because it is mutually agreed to. It is objective, and its sanctions are that if either party withdraws from the contract, the contract no longer exists.

She: Our contract can be broken with breathtaking speed. If you don't pay for a month or if I fail to perform or leave your dirty clothes in a pile where you left them, that's it. And the requirements are simple, clear.

He: Furthermore, there are all sorts of sexual behavior that are not legal.

She: Yes, there are many things a man cannot ask his wife to do because there are other laws forbidding these acts.

He: Therefore, almost every couple that ever drew breath was and is breaking some law.

She: It is assumed in the marriage code that what a woman wants is house, children and comfortable standard of living; what a husband wants is access to her—and some assurance that the children are his. He gives the former to her, and she grants the latter to him. But a man also wants house, children, etc., as well as access. There must have been early trouble when a woman began to wonder if her burden would be lighter, and less hazardous, if she refused the man his "rights." It is assumed by the law that he must provide her with a great deal, and all she has to do is submit.

He: That's a good deal.

She: Wait a minute. Why is the first set of conditions regarded as for her and not for him as well?

He: He has to be the provider of all these things. That can't still be a part of California marital law, can it?

She: California has no-fault divorce now.

He: Presumably you have no-fault marriage, then.

She: I don't know, but I imagine the marriage code is still the same, but the grounds for getting out of marriage are different. The mess reemerges when there are children and you have to determine who is the better parent. If a man fails to provide for the family, the woman can sue for support.

He: But if support still isn't provided, her only recourse is a no-fault divorce. The judge might garnish his wages, but he can't force the man to work. It seems to me it's an unenforceable statute. And with the anti–marital rape statute, a man can't force entry.

She: In most states, a husband can legally force entry.

He: Not in Oregon or in California. Given the fact that all of these laws are more honored in the breach than in the observance, why are they even important or worth discussing? Do you think they actually determine people's behavior?

She: No, no. We were talking about our mistress-master contract and how different it is from a marriage contract. And we now are discovering that it's not that different on paper.

He: The state is not involved, and people do not behave according to the laws that are on the statute books. They might have observed them twenty-five years ago, but they don't now. You were married in California, and none of these things ever occurred to you. Same with me. And in the divorce that I obtained in California, none of these things were ever mentioned.

She: Our thinking about our new contract has been muddled.

He: I'm sure. Practically everything I say is muddled.

DINNER

She: In the late '40s, in the graduate student world, the shared perception of any male and female who went into marriage was fidelity.

He: It was?

She: It certainly was. Otherwise, why marry?

He: How come, to the best of my knowledge, few people practiced it? I don't even recall anyone defending it. In fact, in the late '40s, [we] practically invented open marriage, without ever getting credit for having done so.

She: I don't know why anyone would give credit to any little [collegiate] nucleus in the '40s. It was a mess.

He: It might have been a mess, but it was a harbinger of things to come.

She: It was a collection of miserable married people, and the single ones were no better.

He: All I know is that the patterns of behavior there became prevalent in the '60s. We had all the marijuana we wanted to smoke, the cops weren't hassling us. Attitudes toward fidelity, etc., became modes of behavior in the '60s.

She: So marriage, even then, set the couple apart in the midst of forming new forms. Did you devise a mistress concept then?

He: No, not then, but we were already talking about contractual relationships and Congreve's *The Way of the World*, and by the '60s, the group that I was with evolved that idea and M.C. picked our brains and wrote an article for *Harper's* on it.

She: Evolved what?

He: The idea of contracts in marriage or any relationship, but particularly in marriage. A specific contract which set forth all of the expectations for both parties. G. and S. didn't get married, but they wrote a contract.

She: I don't think this discussion is going anywhere. I can't think of any group of people who have so messed up their personal lives as that particular group. It was disastrous. None endured. Except possibly M. and L., and he committed suicide, though that did not necessarily have anything to do with his marriage.

He: Why *did* he commit suicide?

She: Who knows? He was depressed. I'm not interested in that. I have brought up the late '40s in order to try to separate the mistress-master contract from whatever we thought we were getting in the marriage contract.

He: It must be different. It seems to me that we've had an implied contract for years and years. Why have two of the screwed-up generation, as you would say—you've never known more pathetic types—how can you explain our long period of, if not fidelity, certainly commitment to one another? How did that happen?

She: If you lined up all the people from that time who knew either one of us, all of them would be astonished at our endurance, at our sustained high regard for each other, at our still being together, at our caring for three children who weren't yours as well as your own son. Plus caring for a woman who was five hundred miles away. They'd be amazed, unable to believe their ears. Their amazement is a reflection of their shared expectations, their culture.

DINNER

He: Did it ever occur to you, and I'm sure it has because we've talked about it, that the longevity is in some substantial part explained by the fact that we were not together enough of the time to warp each other by a series of compromises?

She: Probably if we added up all of our together time over fifteen years, it would add up to the average time people stayed together in our "culture," which is the length of time those people could bear each other and their own attitudes.

He: But there's a good deal of health in the other arrangement. When we were apart, we did different things, and therefore we were interesting to each other . . . perhaps exasperating . . . but interesting. In addition, there was the sense that we could develop our own talents and attitudes.

She: In my own development as teacher, I would not have liked to have figured in a husband, as well as three children, day after day. As for your business activity, it seems that for you it was completely necessary to throw yourself wholeheartedly into it, not worry about hearth, home, woman, or children. And that's true of all adventurers. Marriage seems to be a way of taming . . .

He: . . . the adventuresome spirit. And what I'm hoping

now is that by dint of hard work and good decisions, I will continue to free enough money for the various activities we want to engage in, and we will buy that same sense of freedom to do what we want to do. Instead of buying it with youth and vigor, we'll pay money so that we still won't be constrained, and if you want to do something, there will be enough money for you to do it. If you decide that going to Dublin is absolutely necessary, you'll go. We'll have the freedom that has always been the possession of the affluent. Vita Sackville-West, Virginia Woolf, Edith Wharton, you've said could behave in ways that the common lot of mankind were not familiar with.

She: Jessamyn West. Her husband was very bush, and he wasn't interested. So what should they have done? Divorce?

He: The uses of apartness. Its function, its value. It is not a negative value. It's something we should undoubtedly preserve and in our living arrangements not allow another to have an oppressive presence. One of the advantages of the idea of your separate studio is that it will be a place where you can sleep and eat, if that's what you need to do.

She: Tomorrow I have some work I want to start. So I probably will not be cooking dinner . . .

He: . . . or even seeing me. . . .

She: I might come down to the apartment late at night and snuggle into bed. It's exciting to know that I can say that.

He: That's right!

She: Even when I've agreed to take care of you, in our

mistress-master contract, I can still say it! Because I work better at night.

He: Also, one of the things you don't like about me is that I ask what you've done lately, what progress you are making. But the other side of the coin is that you know I'll encourage you. I'm only too happy to see you get down to work.

I think that's enough on the theme of apartness, but you might care to examine it further. The uses of apartness. Never underestimate how difficult it is to be apart unless you have money. For instance, the woman who is in the childbearing period—just listen to Loretta Lynn tell about how much apartness the average couple has when they are raising a family on slim rations. None whatsoever.

She: Remember the scene in the movie when he asks, "What have you done today?"

DINNER (MASTECTOMY)

He: You have wondered about the inclusion of a discussion of your mastectomy in this book.

She: I would like to postpone a discussion of that until the day after tomorrow, at eight o'clock, please.

He: Very well.

She: I think the reason I'd like to postpone it is that it tilts, weighs, skews. It confuses the whole picture. Makes our talks Pollock rather than Munch or Van Gogh. It makes us look stranger than we might otherwise.

He: I don't understand.

She: We want the woman to have a quality of every woman in 1985, age over fifty, and for you to have a quality of every man age late sixties in America. To give me a mastectomy robs me of that everywoman quality.

He: It does? Why?

She: Because few women have mastectomies.

He: I thought many had.

She: What is it? One in ten thousand? Or one in ten? I don't know personally anyone else who does.

He: Betty Ford.

She: Shirley Temple. Ingrid Bergman had two. Happy Rockefeller, two.

He: I find that mastectomies are no more than any of the other elements of physical decay. I don't find mastectomies any less attractive than wrinkles and fat deposits and varicose veins. I put it all in the same category. We're coming apart at the seams, literally. I find it absolutely impossible to separate that out as being anything remarkable. It seems to me that it's an easier defect to handle because it's more like an army wound. You're wounded in the war, you lose an arm, you've got a jagged scar across your breastbone, you're gouged out.

She: Look at it from the reader's point of view. A reader visualizes whatever body he or she wants to go with the female voice. It's disconcerting to visualize someone with a missing breast.

He: I don't think that's true. It might be true for females, but I think for most males it's sort of ho-hum.

She: I think possibly most males are being rather gallant.

He: I don't think it's gallant at all. I think that being in good physical shape is more important than whether you've had a mastectomy or not. I believe most males would feel that way. You can be in excellent physical shape as far as muscle tone and the rest is concerned, and mastectomy is irrelevant. The arm or shoulder may be stiff and require exercise to keep it flexible. But I think that this is just something which concerns you and maybe concerns females, and it's conceivable that if I didn't have a penis, or had lost my balls, I would feel the same way. Breasts are not primary sexual organs.

She: Perhaps not primary, but they carry flesh messages. And some men regard them as primary.

He: Whatever some men might regard, it is anatomically the case that they are not. It's all right with me if you leave out the issue of the mastectomy. I think it's of interest at least, but not of great importance. You have a better idea of "dear reader"'s state of mind.

She: In Bel Kaufman's *Love Etc.*, the narrator runs a writer's workshop, and she tells her budding writers over and over again, "I don't care if it happened. Just because it happened doesn't make it fictionally convincing." That's the way I feel about the mastectomy. We have to think about that.

He: You do. I'm indifferent.

She: *I* have to think about whether or not *we* want the spokeswoman to have one breast.

He: If you think that that would make your spokeswoman's stance less effective . . .

She: It makes her odd. I don't mind her being odd in any number of other ways, but having a missing breast makes her mathematically odd.

He: That is odd.

She: Also it places her in the position of having to explain either what the effect on her is or has been, or to explain that it has had no effect. She has to say that the other men in her life have done this or that in regard to the mastectomy.

He: You could include that little part from *Barefoot Boy with Cheek*. He goes to the sorority house and the housekeeper has huge breasts and he stares at them and she says, "Well, young man, haven't you ever seen breasts before?" and he says, "Yes, but always in even numbers." I think that would place it in proper perspective.

She: No matter how much good, healthy thoughts are going around about mastectomies, it is a loss, and the women feel it as loss. They keep a stiff upper lip, and the men are being gallant. I know of no single published negative comment, by males, about a mastectomy. And yet I *know* that there resides in some of them . . .

He: You'd be surprised at how easily you get used to something. Maybe that's what concerns women, the fact that men really don't give that much of a damn.

She: Yet it does seem strange, with all the advertising of breasts, that in her own household, when one comes back from the hospital with only one breast, that there will be no effect on her own husband. She feels something is being hidden from her.

He: But breasts, just regular old ordinary breasts, by the time most women are fifty . . .

She: Mine are just the same.

He: Your one is.

She: They were never much to begin with, and the one remaining hasn't undone its development.

He: That's right. Small-breasted women don't have the problem that large-breasted women have. If you had the choice of having a large, decayed, pendulous bosom . . .

She: Not all small-breasted women. J.'s breasts hung to her waist after one child. Awful! No, I'd rather have one.

He: So you'd rather have one firm breast than two pendulous ones?

She: Yes.

He: Doesn't that put it into perspective?

She: It helps, but I'm worried about the image.

He: Why don't you just say, "Upon due reflection that most women by the time they are my age have breasts which have declined into shapeless blobs of one kind or another . . ."

She: Sour grapes. That's not true. I see women, many women, my age whose breasts look firm. I don't know what they look like without clothes. My sister is older, and her breasts are firm and big.

He: Why don't you try to meet somebody who was part of that big multiphasic examination of women? They examined tens of thousands. You could sort out those over fifty, look at the photos.

She: They took photos?

He: Maybe not, but they'd know, and it would be one way to satisfy your curiosity. It would be one way to convince you that a mastectomy isn't all that can happen to breasts. If you had two breasts, you would still be as body-shy as you are now.

She: Not as much. I never used to mind revealing my top to you in daylight. I think of the premastectomy period as one of relative abandonment, of lack of shyness, compared to what I feel now.

He: I guess you're saying that you'll never get over it.

She: Dunno.

He: This is getting away from the literary questions. Perhaps you don't want the reader to feel sorry for her.

She: That's another aspect of the literary focus. One wonders, "Are they still together because she had a mastectomy? Has he remained responsible for her because of that? Is the mistress-master contract possibly like a slum redevelopment project? Does it originate in some kind of sympathy for her?" Maybe she accepts his freedom to do what he wants because that's all she can ask. Because she only has one breast. I'm trying to think about all this, not only what the reader might think but what may in fact be the case. Are you being noble and virtuous?

He: I don't know. I don't know that about myself. That's why when you suggest that we may have achieved honesty, I laugh. How would I know? We're together, from my viewpoint, because I find you interesting and I love to screw you and I keep trying to get us to the point of a remembered sexual compatibility. We've worked back and forth, literally, for three years on this, and it seems more satisfactory now than it has been.

She: There are any number of reasons besides one-breastedness that would justify your exit. I cost too much, I'm hard to get along with sometimes. You might find another woman. And if you did leave, I would not say to myself that it was because, alas, I only had one breast. I don't believe that you're wholly good and virtuous. You're also a softy.

He: Remember the first night we slept together postmastectomy, and you had constructed a sash that fit over the wound? And what was my response? "Take it off." When you resisted, I said, "Take it off, now. I want you, not the goddamned sash."

She: I had to comply.

He: That's right. Here I have all of these property rights, and I'm still having trouble exercising them.

She: Yes; what did you mean yesterday when you said you were shy? You said it was like being a young kid again. What did you mean?

He: Here I know I can do anything I want with you . . .

She: But you're shy about doing it? What do you want to do?

He: My thoughts come to all sorts of bizarre things, and I think, "No. that wouldn't go over very well."

She: Because you've never had a property?

He: That's right.

She: You didn't feel that way in marriage?

He: No, no. No matter what the law might have said. And I realize that you probably are waiting for me to utilize you as a property . . . if for nothing else, the literary material. . . .

She: (*Laughter*) I'm sure you spend at least part of your time at the office figuring it out. You don't, do you? On the freeway?

He: I know you wonder what I'll come up with.

She: Only because I think the word "property" will suggest things to you . . . rather different than the words "my own true love."

He: And vice versa, right?

She: There's a difference between us: I can't imagine your being my property. I can own a house and allow the weeds to take over. I can do nothing to it and feel quite comfortable doing nothing. But you, you put irrigation systems in, put goats on the land to devour poison oak. Being an improving landlord excites you.

He: You want a good master, don't you?

She: Yes—last night was fun. The best thing about last night was that I thought we were working on your back. . . .

He: Until I turned on you. But you must have wondered what the double-headed vibrator would feel like, didn't you?

She: Sure, but I didn't know you were going to do it. I thought you were sick.

He: I was! And it did help my head. I want you to work on my back again.

BED

She: Sh-h-h. Let me say it, and then you can talk. The more I try to be what you want me to be (a sexy lady, etc.)—to meet your standards, which are high (as your energy is high for all things), to fulfill your hopes (which are mine but seem impossible to accomplish)—the less I am what you want me to be and the more off-center I feel. The day starts with the knowledge that I have fallen short and gets worse from then on.

He: I don't want to be the controller of you. I want us to do our work, to get on with it, and to enjoy our time together.

She: Yes, but often I feel that you are wasting your talents on a perverse female body which does all right in fantasy but feels suffocated and anaesthetized by your intentions. I dreamt night before last that you turned away from me to another woman who gave you what you need, want, and can use.

He: I don't *want* any other woman.

She: I could only watch the transfer and weep. Sometimes my fear is so dense it becomes my weather, my element.

He: I certainly have no intention of producing fear. That's terrible! Last night, when you came to my apartment, I suggested we should call off sex, build separate dwellings instead of a beautiful house; we should have dinner together and then part, coming together only when we (that is, *you*) feel desire. I was opposing your all-is-lost face with the purest rationality.

She: Yes, you presented a plan. I said, "We want to create a beautiful house in which we shall stalk each other." Do you remember what happened next?

He: I'm not likely to forget an occasion when the habit of a lifetime, the requirement of my male condition, was so softly, firmly reversed. Yes, I presented my plan, which I thought had all the virtue of altering what was for you an intolerable situation, and you said, your face sad but serene, "Let's go to bed."

She: And you said, "All right. I'll pack up my budgets and we'll go get something to eat and then . . ."

He: Knowing you to be a lady of ritual—first dinner, *then* retiring—I thought I knew what you meant. But you said, "No, let's go to bed now."

She: And you replied, "Now? That's fine. We'll drive to your place. We can have crackers and soup there."

He: But you fired back, in a whisper, "Now. In your bedroom." Again, you gave me no clue to your feelings. Perhaps I can be excused for believing that your invitation was a forcing, that your will was leading you and no good could come of it.

She: And then what happened?

He: Then, my sweet lady, forgive the expression, you fucked me.

She: I don't forgive the expression. I made love to you, and if I remember rightly, I had to stop your talk with kisses. You never used to be so talky in bed. In fact, that was part of your magic, that you said nothing.

He: It's the fault of the book. How is the reader to know the conceptual forms of our search if we do not translate?

She: Quite inappropriately, you continued with your plans. I had no choice.

He: Although you stopped my tongue, I continued to analyze and wondered if suddenly you had became a great actress, simulating passion and an ardor such as I'd seldom, if ever, experienced, and never one which flowed in my direction without at least some priming. My last thought, early on, was "If she's faking it, she'll have a terrible hangover before midnight!"

She: To save you the trouble of pointing it out, I controlled the lovemaking and enjoyed every minute.

He: Yes, and that included doing things like sucking me and being entered from the rear, which have never failed, in the past, to arouse in you a veritable hailstorm of resentment.

She: I wanted to. And you are not to conclude that henceforth I must be in charge.

He: You want me to keep my conclusions to myself?

She: For the time being.

He: Afterwards, you said to me, "I want to love men. That is what feminism has brought me. I have received all of the messages, and I want to love men."